QUEEN OF DIAMONDS

The baseball story of Kenosha's Joyce Westerman

With Randy Donais
Forward by Pastor Stacy Seger

Zeta Publishing
Ocala, FL

Copyright © 2017 by Randy Donais

All rights reserved. No part of this publication may be reproduced, distributed, or transmitted in any form or by any means, including photocopying, recording, or other electronic or mechanical methods, without the prior written permission of the publisher, except in the case of brief quotations embodied in critical reviews and certain other noncommercial uses permitted by copyright law. For permission requests, write to the publisher, addressed "Attention: Permissions Coordinator," at the address below.

Zeta Publishing, Inc
3850 SE 58th Ave
Ocala, FL 34480
www.zetapublishing.com

Ordering Information:
Quantity sales. Special discounts are available on quantity purchases by corporations, associations, and others. For details, contact the publisher at the address above.
Orders by U.S. trade bookstores and wholesalers. Please contact Zeta Publishing: Tel: (352) 694-2553; Fax: (352) 694-1791 or visit www.zetapublishing.com

ISBN: 978-1-947191-56-3 (sc)

ISBN: 978-1-947191-57-0 (e)

Library of Congress Control Number: 2017961577

Printed in the United States of America

Table of Contents

Forward by Pastor Stacy Seger, Lord of Life Lutheran Church..............vii
Meet Joyce Westerman, by Randy Donais..ix
Chapter 1: The Early Years..1
Chapter 2: Life In The AAGPBL..9
Chapter 3: The 1952 Season 19
Chapter 4: Life After The AAGPBL...27
Chapter 5: A League Of Big Names...35
Chapter 6: Yes, Women Can Play This Game....................................41
Chapter 7: If You Like Numbers here's some more..........................47
Chapter 8: Managers..51
Chapter 9: More History..57
Chapter 10: How It All Began..63
Chapter 11: A League of Their Own..73
Chapter 12: They Said It..79
Chapter 13: More Facts And Numbers 83
Chapter 14: Some Final Thoughts...87

Forward

As a pastor, I am blessed to meet amazing and interesting people every day. The stories that people carry with them are simply fascinating. There are few stories that have captivated me more than Joyce Hill Westerman's.

We all have dreams; big and little. It takes an extra dose of courage and a whole heap of chutzpah to make them a reality. Joyce has both in abundance! When I first became the pastor at Joyce's church, Lord of Life Lutheran in Kenosha, WI, she quickly invited me out for lunch so we could get to know one another. Over a couple of patty melts she told me about her growing up in the area and her time playing professional baseball. There was a twinkle in her eyes and energy in her voice that was much younger than her 85+ years!

One weekend afternoon Joyce invited my family and I to her home. We shared a meal and she tossed a baseball around the backyard with our then 2-year old son, Sam. The highlight of our day was the time we spent in her spare room – looking through the treasures of her time in professional baseball. There were trading cards (which I have a signed copy of proudly displayed in our home), game programs, pennants, posters and uniforms. One of her prized possessions stood prominently on the middle table – a display case she had specially made to hold baseballs. Inside was a ball from every year she had played. At the end of each season, she asked all of her teammates and coaches to sign a ball that she held on to. These balls were displayed with pride. They stand as a tribute to all the people who journeyed with Joyce through her life.

Joyce had a dream – she often refers to her time playing baseball as a "dream come true" – and she knows that dreams don't come true for everyone or on their own. Throughout her life, she was surrounded by a village that held her up and moved her forward; her family, her friends, her teammates … all of them played a role in helping her dream to come true. What a joy to read this book filled with stories of the village that surrounded Joyce! God has surely blessed her with an amazing village – God has surely blessed us with Joyce Hill Westerman!

In gratitude & with joy!

Rev Stacy Seger Pastor,
Lord of Life Lutheran Church
Kenosha, WI

Meet Joyce Westerman
Summer, 2017

In my mind Joyce Hill-Westerman is not a hero. In Joyce's mind she is not one, either. The 91-year-old veteran of eight seasons in the All-American Girls Professional Baseball League bristles when somebody suggests she is. "I am not a hero! I used to feel embarrassed when somebody said that." she said in a recent interview. "I was no better than anybody else.". I have to agree with Joyce 100 percent. She was an average player in the AAGPBL and had to work hard to be one. Joyce went out a champion. She went from bench warmer in 1945 to MVP candidate of the 1952 championship series. Joyce is no stranger to hard work. Since her parents lost their home in the Roosevelt School neighborhood in Kenosha, Wisconsin Joyce's life has been in beast mode to the present day. This is a story of perseverance if there ever was one.

Jerry Kramer, the former offensive guard of the Green Bay Packers during the Vince Lombardi era who should be in the National Football League's Hall of Fame, probably said it best. **"The harder**

Randy Donais

I worked the luckier I got." When I think of Jerry Kramer I think of Joyce. Both of them are incredibly blessed for different reasons and in different ways. Both of them walked away from the games they loved winners, champions. And both are equally successful as people long after they played. The things I love about Joyce is her consistency as a person. Her character and work ethic are unequaled and have remained the same her entire life. This little woman still cuts her one acre-plus yard twice a week on a riding mower and shovels snow off of her two car wide driveway! Every summer she gets on a short ladder and washes her outside windows. She washes her car by hand and rides her exercise bike every morning.

Joyce's back bothers her and walks with a cane. Her hearing is not good. In 2000 she had two open heart surgeries four months apart yet still helped out on the AAGPBL reunion at Milwaukee County Stadium that summer. Her gall bladder removal years ago wasn't pretty. And to this day Joyce Westerman continues to persist. "You know, Randy." she told me not long ago. "You're here today, gone tomorrow." Joyce weighs about 114 pounds (she played at about 150 pounds) yet she dives into the treats which are served after every Sunday morning service. She also loves the soup suppers on Wednesday nights during Lent. Joyce's youngest daughter Judy comes over whenever she can help. Many times the two women will share a simple meal. Joyce confessed she is slowing down. And at 91 who wouldn't? "Just a few years ago I was fine." she said. "I do need some help now with the outside stuff." Don't kid yourselves! This woman is still tough as nails! If you don't think so shake hands with her! She still drives around town and does her own shopping. Attending the morning service every Sunday at Lord of Life Lutheran Church is a top priority. Joyce has been fiercely independent her entire life and "probably more so" since her husband Ray passed away just before Christmas in 2005. Before you judge Joyce or even myself read this book in its entirety and decide for yourself!

Queen of Diamonds

Pastor Stacy Seger and Joyce's friend June Pomatto at Lord of Life call her "amazing". Joyce is mother of two, grandmother of eight and great-grandmother of three. Two Christmas Eves ago she had 23 people over to her modest north side home. Try pulling that off just days before your 90th birthday! "I had a little bit of help." she admitted. Before I started writing this book I tried to count the roles Joyce has played in her life: friend, wife, mother, grandmother, daughter, niece, aunt, sister, co-worker, teammate, catcher, first baseman, left fielder, clutch hitter, 4H leader, and school board member, reunion contributor and Hall of Famer!

Yes, her name is on a bronze plaque in the AAGPBL wing of Baseball's Hall of Fame, the very same shrine that houses baseball's immortals. Joyce also made a brief appearance in the 1992 movie "A League of Their Own", but don't call her an actress! Most definitely, don't call her a hero! Those who were close to Joyce knew her as one of the leaders and backbones in the AAGPBL, which after 65 years since she last collected a paycheck, is still very special to her. You can't help but like Joyce. She is about as affable, humble and easy going as they come. Every where you look she attracts quality people to her. Legend? Read the entire book and you tell me! "Oh, I don't know! I suppose!" she blushed. Nothing is out of place in Joyce's meticulously clean home. One of the extra bedrooms looks like an AAGPBL museum. Needless to say Joyce is in constant motion always doing something. She doesn't have cable or satellite TV but likes watching the Green Bay Packers or a Major League Baseball game on a network channel. This is a woman who would rather talk about life in the AAGPBL than her personal accomplishments. You don't have to twist Joyce's arm if you want to sit and talk baseball over a latte or ice cream cone at McDonald's. She has a lot of memories which I will share in this book. Joyce doesn't remember everything but remembers more than I hoped for.

Most of this book is through her eyes but I got a lot of help from other sources and they will be acknowledged in the end.

Joyce played the middle eight years of the league's 12-year existence, primarily as a catcher. She speaks respectfully of her time in the league and the people in it. She admits that playing in the AAGPBL was not as glamorous as "A League Of Their Own" made it out to be.

"About 80 percent accurate." she once said.

Joyce was at the Baseball Hall of Fame in Cooperstown, New York in 1988 when the league was officially recognized with a huge bronze plaque with the players' names inscribed on it. Every player and manager who played or served significantly is on it. The league of their own now has a wing of their own in baseball heaven. I will talk more about the movie later in this book. Most of the girls (15-28) who made a team in 1943 were paid between $50 and $85 a week. Not bad pay during the World War II and then Korean Conflict eras. In 2017 that translates between $625 and $1,200 a week It was written back during the war years that male bread winners would have been thrilled to bring home that kind of money. Joyce's best salary was in 1952, her last season in the league, when she "held out" and received $110 a week! That's $440 a month! No agent! Needless to say the South Bend Blue Sox wanted Joyce pretty badly and it turned out to be one of the smartest moves its brain trust ever made. That shows the respect Joyce had in the league. To the Blue Sox it was money well spent since Joyce came up clutch time and again in the AAGPBL playoffs. With Joyce leading the way the Blue Sox became league champions for the second straight year.

Joyce just wanted to play. Those uniform dresses were hard enough to play in, let alone catch in, which few girls were willing to try. "I learned how to catch on the fly more or less." Joyce said. "Yeh, they (teammates) had some disputes with managers. I was quiet. I got along with all of them (teammates and managers). I didn't want to get kicked off the team." Joyce threw right and batted left. She was a line drive spray hitter who tried to "hit them where they weren't".

Looking and carrying themselves like young ladies was as important as softball/baseball ability. "Some of the girls were really attractive." She recalled. "Then there were girls like me who were athletic." They were ladies first and foremost until they heard the screams from the dugout "Dirt in the skirt!" While stealing a base or sliding into third with a triple.

Joyce certainly wasn't Johnny Bench or even Bob Uecker. She didn't have Hall of Fame numbers but was one of the AAGPBL's hardest workers. Her lifetime batting average was .227 (345 hits in 1,515 official plate appearances). The league average, according to the AAGPBL website, was a shade under .202. There were home run hitters in the league but Joyce didn't have the home run stroke. "I didn't run very well but I hit a lot of gappers." Joyce once said. Joyce is not into self-promotion but loves talking about life in the league for which she "left it all out on the field". And again, playing in the AAGPBL wasn't very glamorous, but her hard work paid off by way of a league championship in her final season. Joyce has no regrets. "It was a dream come true." She said. "It was the best thing that happened to me except for my family."

The Early Years
Chapter 1

Joyce was somebody who would not be denied anything. Even as a young woman she could have been a motivational speaker teaching a board room full of sales people how to set a goal and achieve it. Joyce made it happen for herself time and again. She did not grow up as they say "with a silver spoon in her mouth". She was born Joyce Elaine Hill on December 29, 1925, the fourth of eight children to Cecil Ludlow-Hill and Lillian Clausen-Hill. Four girls and four boys, although one boy died at birth. Only one of Joyce's sisters, Evelyn Schaefer, and one of her brothers, Richard Hill, are still with us.

When Joyce was about five the Hill family was hit hard by the Great Depression as Cecil and Lillian lost their Kenosha home in the Roosevelt School neighborhood. Cecil toiled away at Nash Motors in the middle of Kenosha, which was later called American Motors and then Chrysler Motors. When the Stock Market Crash of 1929 hit people lost their jobs and thus did not have the money to buy new cars. Unfortunately, the Hills felt the crunch like everybody else.

Cecil got laid off. So the family moved out to where the Pleasant Prairie Power Plant is today.

Joyce's uncle George Clausen leased two acres of his maternal grandparents' original 80-acre farm to Cecil and Lillian. The beginnings were as humble as one could imagine. "There was no water, no electricity, no plumbing, no nothing." said Joyce. "We had an old (pot belly) stove and that was about it. We didn't have a washer or dryer but we did have a ringer. That's the way it was until I went to Lincoln Junior High." Before seventh grade the family moved into the upstairs of a much nicer house on the other side of the 80-acre homestead.

Joyce fed the steers and some of the smaller farm creatures while living in the old house. When she moved to the other side of the homestead her work load increased. Joyce attended a one-room school house called the Starr School in Pleasant Prairie. Her two daughters also went there about 30 years later. During that time she also sat on the school board for about five years. She personified the Hill work ethic as the family dug themselves out of a deep hole. Everybody worked hard, especially Joyce, who did everything she was asked to do and then some on the farm. "I fed the steers, the cows, the chickens, the pigs and horses." she recalled. "You name it I did it." And that included filling crates and wagons full of vegetables, fruit and hay and learning how to drive the tractor before she was 15. There was much more work on the other side of the 80. She even cleaned the barns.

The family saw light at the end of the tunnel. Cecil planted more crops and bought more livestock, even turkeys. He was called back to Nash which made things much easier financially. Joyce said her father did little on the farm once he went back to work. Joyce and her three older sisters -- Evelyn, Lorraine and Marguerite – did most of the work inside since they were the four oldest. The three boys – Cecil, George and Richard – were still young and did little. "Aside from working he didn't do all that much." Joyce said of her dad once he came home. All seven kids were accountable for something every day.

Joyce and two of her older sisters got an early ride into Kenosha every morning since Cecil had to start work at 7 a.m. Joyce was in seventh grade at Lincoln Junior High, her two older sisters at Kenosha High School. The hard working Joyce achieved a measure of success by purchasing a bicycle for five dollars. Joyce earned the money cutting down weeds and thickets for a "future brother-in-law" on a "truck farm" in Somers for 10 cents an hour. The bike was actually purchased from a private party in Kenosha. There wasn't much in the line of entertainment for Joyce. She listened to the Chicago Cubs on one of those old fashioned box radios when she wasn't in school and joined 4-H when she was nine. "That was the only other thing we had for entertainment was 4-H." She said. Back then, of course, the Cubs played all of their home games in the afternoon as did every one of their opponents. Night baseball was on the horizon. Joyce was unbelievably busy but listened when she could. It was becoming quite clear she was taking a serious interest in baseball. "I don't know. I must've grown up with it." Joyce recalled. "We had a radio so I listened to the Cubs." The only other things Joyce did was read and play with the other children if they happened to be in the area. Life on the farm was making her stronger and she could outhit many of the boys out in the pasture or in sand lot games. There were no Milwaukee Braves, Brewers or Minnesota Twins in the early 1930's. The Chicago White Sox were and still are about 10 miles south of the Cubs but it was the Cubs' signal Joyce picked up on the family radio.

Then one summer day in 1933 changed Joyce's life forever. Her aunt and uncle, Mabel Clausen-Anderson and Albert Anderson, decided to take their seven and a half year old niece down to Chicago to attend a Cubs game. "They (her family) thought it would be a nice idea so we drove down." Joyce said. "I remember being really excited." When they got down near what is today Wrigleyville Joyce recalled "not having to walk very far" from a parking spot on a street. She also experienced the sights and smells of a big league ball park – vendors, cigar smoke, popcorn, hot dogs and stale beer. A day at the ballpark back then was almost a guy thing.

The Cubs did not sell out very often even though they had a good team during the Depression/Prohibition years. Today every game is sold out and has been for years. Joyce doesn't remember how much the tickets cost but the average seat was a couple of bucks or less. Bleacher seats were two bits. The Cubs were coming off a tough World Series loss to the New York Yankees the previous season. Babe Ruth was said to have pointed to the centerfield bleachers with two called strikes on him then deposited the third pitch in that direction for a tremendous home run. At least legend had it. So the Andersons and their young niece sat on the third base side. Joyce was excited to finally see the faces and uniform numbers she only heard about on the radio. "I don't remember who won or lost or who the Cubs played." Joyce said. Unfortunately she does not remember the month or day. "I was just excited to be there."

Joyce remembered watching the tail end of batting practice. She also remembered being in awe at what it was like to watch a baseball sail into the bleachers. The ivy-colored walls were in full bloom and waving in the breeze. Back then catcher Gabby Hartnett was the Cubs' best player. He was the leader behind the plate handling pitchers and making sure everybody was on the same page defensively. The 6-foot-1, 195-pound Hartnett carried a potent bat and was in the prime of a Hall of Fame career. He was voted baseball's top catcher for the first 50 years of the 20th century. Said Joyce "I like the way he threw the ball to second and just the way he moved around out there." Joyce doesn't recall attending very many major league games in future years but Hartnett put the seed in her mind. It wasn't long before Joyce began to play in county and city girls and women's leagues. After watching Hartnett play she wanted to catch. "I pitched for awhile and let me tell you I was no pitcher." she said. "I liked catching the best so I started catching all the time." Even at a young age Joyce proved she could play with the big girls. "I was really young, 10 or 11 years old." she said. "My aunt's (Esther Clausen) city league team was called the Lincoln Stars. Sometimes they let me catch."

Joyce played with her aunt's team and later the Nash city league team when she went to work for Nash. The best women's team in town was the Ken-Nash-A team and it played its games at the Nash Employees Athletic Field on the southeast corner of 30th Avenue and 52nd Street. That's the team Joyce wanted to play for and that's the park she wanted to play in.

The Nash Field was clearly Kenosha's premier field early in the 20th century. It briefly hosted professional football in 1924. It opened in 1923. "I always wanted to play there." recalled Joyce. Simmons Field opened in 1920 and Lakefront Stadium in 1937. Heck, a Kenosha News article written after the Cubs' World Series win in 2016 said the 1908 Cubs were set to travel to Kenosha for an exhibition game against a local team. The game never took place citing an ordinance prohibiting organized sporting events on Sundays. There was no high school softball teams back then but Joyce kept playing and getting better. The ladies' game was strictly fast pitch softball, not baseball.

After graduating from high school in June, 1943 Joyce continued to play. She was determined to land a job with Nash and play on its team. So much so she made a pest of herself at the employment office daily until she got hired. A lot of guys from out of town tried to get jobs and the guys who were laid off wanted their jobs back. But Joyce would not be denied. Instead of building cars, which weren't selling, Nash focused on building airplane engines. Unfortunately, Nash Field had to be sacrificed about 1942 so that factory space could be created for airplane engine production.

Joyce's job was polishing engine pistons. Not a strenuous job, she said, but monotonous. Joyce was a gamer so she did it. She wanted to make money like everybody else. Soon after the war ended on August 14, 1945 Nash returned to the production of cars. Joyce continued to make money working at Nash during her off seasons. Later in 1945 Joyce bought a brand new Nash Ambassador 4-door for $345. Remembering what happened to her mom and dad when she was young Joyce paid cash. She would have no part of taking out a loan or having to owe anybody anything. She still believes in that today.

After graduating from high school Joyce worked at Nash all that summer.

In the spring of 1944 she was asked to try out as a fill in for the Kenosha Comets. Joyce and Ruth Radatz were chosen out of about two dozen girls to fill in for about three weeks until the regulars recovered from their injuries. Joyce recalled making one pinch hitting appearance. Joyce and Ruth did not get paid but the experience was priceless. "I don't remember getting (paid) anything." she said. Later that summer Joyce was sent to Racine to try out as a fill in with the Belles. That's where she spent the rest of the 1944 season.

The All-American Girls Professional Baseball League began play in June of 1943 and the Comets and Belles were two of the four charter teams. The other two were the Rockford Peaches and South Bend Blue Sox. "I didn't know much about the (AAGPBL) league. All I remember is that Kenosha had a team." Joyce said. "They needed two players because of injuries or whatever so they asked us to fill in."

Back then the Belles played at Racine's Horlick Field, the Comets at Lakefront Stadium in Kenosha.

During the winter of 1944-45 Joyce got the call from the AAGPBL to try out for a permanent roster spot the following spring in Chicago. "How they got my (phone) number I'll never know." recalled Joyce. "I was scared stiff to go down there. I hardly went out of Kenosha. I remember somebody met me at the (train) station." It should be noted Ruth Radatz's life went in a different direction. "She was really a good hitter." Said Joyce. And Ruth turned out to be a really good civil servant for the City of Kenosha.

Ruth was President of the Kenosha Common Council from 1972 to 1988 and once filled in for the vacationing Wallace Burkee as mayor in 1972. She also served on the School Board between 1986 and 1989 and was Kenosha County Treasurer/Clerk. Joyce remembers staying at the Belmont Hotel during her three-week spring training stay in Chicago. Competition began at Wrigley Field then moved to a city field and south for a series of exhibition games. When the league was first launched the girls actually played fast pitch softball. The pitching distance between the rubber and home plate was 40 feet. The bases were 65 feet apart and the ball 12 inches in circumference.

Toward the end of the league's existence in the early 50's the game looked more like baseball. The game went from the fast pitch delivery to sidearm/three quarters to overhand with each stage using a smaller ball. The pitching distance toward the end of the league was 60 feet, bases 85 feet apart. Technically, there was a salary cap every year. It started at about $5,000 a month for 15 girls per team to almost $5,500 a month for 18 girls per team toward the end of the league's existence. Some teams had a hard time paying their girls on time because of poor promotion and spotty attendance. The league tried its best to balance out talent and salary. There was no such thing as job security for anybody. And there was no such thing as guaranteed or multi-year contracts.

Joyce was traded four times and played for five different franchises in eight years. Except for a few exceptions the game's best players were traded at least once. When the league first started everybody was paid about the same but it wasn't long before the better players got paid the best. Joyce's best salary was $440 a month in 1952, her last year. The best salaries were in the $700 a month range. There were no agents, no benefits to speak of, no players association until 1988 and little negotiating. The girls were taken care of on the road, but not much else in addition to their player salaries. "They (ballclub) sent you a contract." Joyce recalled. "Either you signed it or you didn't."

After three weeks of spring training the 19-year-old Joyce Hill made the cut and was signed by the Grand Rapids Chicks, who won the league championship the year before as the Milwaukee Chicks.

Life In The AAGPBL
Chapter 2

As the league began its third season in 1945 there were now eight teams. Of all the softball playing girls in the United States and southern Canada Joyce had one of 120 roster spots in the fledging new professional league. It wasn't much fun for Joyce at first as she did a lot of sitting and learning. She understood she had to be ready when her chance came. Joyce found out soon she also needed a sense of humor. Jo Kabick, one of Joyce's older teammates on the Chicks, and another girl decided to have some fun with the rookie.

The three players went to a drive in and ordered ice cream, one of Joyce's guilty pleasures, which was almost as important as playing. When Kabick and the other girl brought Joyce's dish of ice cream to her a short distance away from the counter Joyce took one slurp and spit it out. Instead of sprinkles the ice cream was loaded with salt. Joyce went ballistic. "They found out what a temper I had." she said. "I told them in no uncertain terms not to do that again."

When Joyce wasn't playing it felt more like a job than a game. "A lot of the girls from California and down south played all the time." She said. "Not here in Wisconsin. I had to work hard to earn my spot." Joyce kept pretty much to herself not wishing to say something she might regret. She did speak when spoken to yet continued to work hard on her craft. It would be an understatement to say Joyce's career was off to a slow start as she played for three teams in less than two seasons.

The positive was somebody always saw the potential in Joyce. A good catcher was hard to come by since many of the girls disliked putting on the tools of ignorance. Plus, Joyce was a gamer and left-handed swinger. All she could do was stay with it. "I caught batting practice. I did as much as I could." she said. "I don't think anybody worked harder than I did." Almost all of the managers had years of professional experience but Joyce said rarely did they provide personal instruction. "Not a lot of coaches (managers) took you aside and told you this or showed you that." She said. "I think they figured you should know how to play the game at that level." Each team had 15 players, a manager, business manager, chaperone, but no coaches, trainers, equipment managers or team doctors when the league started.

The following season, 1946, Joyce was looking forward to being the Kenosha Comets' opening day catcher when she was traded to South Bend two days prior. Toward the end of the season she was traded to Fort Wayne "for three weeks to help them out". Joyce would only say about the trade to Fort Wayne, "I wasn't very happy about it." There was one highlight during Joyce's first tour of duty in South Bend. The Blue Sox's Fourth of July doubleheader against Kenosha at Playland Field in South Bend was said to have attracted a league record 10,000 fans. There was no way to tell for sure since seating did not accommodate that many fans. "All I remember was there was a lot of people." said Joyce. "Once you get on the field and play you don't pay any attention to that."

Joyce also had to deal with some injuries – a broken nose, broken finger and sprained ankle. Per diem money in the league was five dollars a day per player on the road. "A dollar back then got you a pretty good meal." Joyce recalled. "I was saving money because I knew I was going to get married." After the 1946 season ended Joyce met her future husband Ray Westerman in Kenosha. "He was working with my sister Evelyn at Nash." recalled Joyce. "We met at this place called Burt's out near the interstate. He was a nice guy so the girls invited him out to a dance." So Joyce and Ray stayed close even though Joyce's summers were booked up playing professional softball, then baseball.

Each girl was given a home and road uniform called a tunic which looked like a combination of tennis, figure skating and field hockey outfits. It was a short-sleeve-like dress with the hem not supposed to be more than six inches above the knee. The material was a heavy twill for rugged endurance but not very comfortable in the summer heat. Every girl wore a hat and a belt. The name of the team was on a circular patch sewn on the uniform in the sternum area.

Joyce said the chaperones washed the uniforms on the road. Besides washing uniforms chaperones were supposed to make sure the girls dressed and acted like ladies on and off the field. Although it wasn't technically their job sometimes the girls needed a woman to talk to about things they couldn't talk to the manager about. "They (chaperones) washed our uniforms. We had to wash our own underwear and socks." Joyce said.

There were curfews on the road depending on when the game ended. Some girls smoked cigarettes, drank more than they were supposed to and flirted with the opposite sex, all no-nos. It wasn't like they weren't all business on the field but as Cindy Lauper sang it, "Girls just want to have fun!". There were no performance enhancing drugs back them and Joyce did not recall seeing anybody get high. Girls were supposed to wear dresses or skirts at all times. The girls had to purchase their own spikes. A lot of girls chose spikes which resembled saddle shoes. "They were all right. They fit like regular shoes." She said. "They were steel spikes."

Travel wasn't all that pretty. Car, bus and occasionally train were the modes of travel depending where teams were playing and how much time they had in between games. There were no corporate jets or luxury buses. Somebody either brought a harmonica or guitar on road trips. Some played cards, others slept or wrote letters. All the teams played within two hours of Chicago. It should be noted teams visited veteran hospitals and UFO posts whenever possible. They were the All-American girls and the league encouraged that. Joyce remembered it was sometimes tough finding time to eat. There was no such thing as fast food back then. Every once in awhile the girls ate at a nice family restaurant otherwise it was greasy spoons and roadside diners.

Speaking of pressed for time. It wasn't unusual for the girls to have to change in to their uniforms on the bus or in the cars before getting to the ballpark with little time to warm up. "And sometimes we had to play in the same uniform two or three days in a row." Said Joyce. It was nice for Joyce to sleep in her own bed in Pleasant Prairie whenever her team played in Kenosha or Racine. The people who handled the accounting loved it since it saved the team a little on the hotel/motel bill. When Joyce's team came to town she would take them to the farm where they got a good home cooked meal from Lillian. It also afforded her some time to be with Ray, who was a supervisor at Nash.

There were some other pluses to life in the AAGPBL. One of the fans, supporters or owners had the girls over for an occasional cookout or took them out to a nice restaurant. That did not happen often, though. Cecil and Lillian sometimes attended games and brought along a basket of goodies for Joyce. When I attended Wisconsin-Whitewater my folks called it "a CARE package". "Whenever I played in Kenosha and Racine they usually came." she said. And Joyce recalled her folks tried to make the long drive to Peoria at least once a year.

Joyce appeared in 531 games in eight seasons. Early on it was the manager's decision not to play her. When she got the chance to play the injury bug bit. Chaperones carried a first aid kit for scrapes or cuts. If an injury was more serious than that, Joyce said, they had to hope a doctor was in attendance or a hospital nearby. "We didn't play on the best fields," Joyce said. She could not remember one worse than another. "One time I was in the outfield during batting practice and I stepped in a rabbit hole and sprained my ankle." Another time Joyce was warming up a pitcher between innings. A hot dog named Fay Dancer, a teammate of Joyce's at the time, was told to jump in the batter's box as if the game had resumed. Joyce was not wearing her mask and took a foul tip right on the nose. "She was a showman." Joyce said. "She used to do cartwheels in center field and wave to the fans." Joyce got over it as she and Dancer became friends. In addition to the aforementioned injuries Joyce got spiked costing her more playing time. Joyce recalled another time she was playing left field when she misjudged a fly ball that almost hit her in the head. Fly balls and pop ups were an adventure if there was a "high sky" on a cloudless day or a night game at a park with poor lighting. "I started wearing glasses after that." She said. "I just couldn't see the ball coming down."

Travel to and from spring training sites was paid for by the league. Wrigley Field, Peru, Illinois, Havana, Cuba, French Lick, Indiana, Miami, Florida, Opa Locka, Florida, Alexandria, Virginia and Pascagoula, Mississippi (not all in that order) were the sites, some of them twice. Not only was the weather better in the spring but the league had thoughts of possibly expanding into the south. Making money and saving money were always motivating factors for the girls.

Some saved up for college, some saved up to help out at home and others, like Joyce, saved up to get married. "A lot of girls did that." She said. "I thought about going to college. I didn't take the right subjects. If I had the right desire I could've worked it out." Even though Joyce was making decent money playing ball she tried to work as much as she could in the off season. "Whenever I could I tried to make a few bucks for Christmas even though I lived at home." She said. "You name it I worked there; Nash, Cooper, Jockey, Simmons.".. And even at the sauerkraut plant in Franksville in Racine County. Joyce was primarily a catcher but played some outfield and first base on some of the teams she played on. She was versatile and managers liked that.

She thought she would get a chance to play regularly in 1946 when she was traded to Fort Wayne. She sat the bench virtually that entire season and was traded again to Fort Wayne for the final three weeks of the season. Joyce appeared in just nine games for the Chicks in 1945 and 21 for the Blue Sox and Daisies in 1946. She went to bat 18 times with the Chicks and managed to get her first two professional hits. "My first hit was just a single but it felt like a home run." She recalled. There were some laughs to be had during spring training. One in particular came in 1946 in Pascagoula. The girls trained on an army base near the Gulf of Mexico and stayed in a hotel near by. "We called it the Cockroach Hotel on Cockroach Boulevard." Said Joyce. "You could hear them running around on the floor. When we turned on the light they all scattered."

The following spring in Havana Joyce thought about quitting. "That was the one time I thought about quitting (in 1947)." she said. "I was beginning to wonder if it was all worth it." As the style and format of the game slowly transcended from softball to baseball Joyce got better and played more regularly. Getting out from behind the plate also helped. "The pitching was difficult." She said. "It was faster when it was underhand (fast pitch style)." Joyce hung in there.

Johnny Gottselig, a two-time Stanley Cup champion with the Chicago Blackhawks, managed Joyce in Peoria in 1947 and gave her a chance to play regularly. "A lot of the girls didn't like him." said Joyce. "But he encouraged me." In 1947 Joyce appeared in 90 games for the Red Wings and batted a respectable .227 on 57 hits and 19 runs batted in. She also walked 36 times. Between 1947 and 1951 Joyce spent her time either playing for Peoria or Racine. After Gottselig moved on baseball lifer Leo Schrall took over in Peoria in 1948. Joyce played most of that season in Peoria thinking she was finally playing on a winning team. As fate would have it Joyce was traded from one winning team to another that being the Belles who swept the Red Wings in the playoffs. "He had a good temperament and treated us fairly." said Joyce of Schrall. Not only did the Belles have a good team but Joyce again was able to sleep at home in Pleasant Prairie. She did have to say good bye to her three roommates in Peoria who were also among her best friends. Between the two teams Joyce got into 89 games and totaled 47 hits, 43 walks, 28 RBI and 29 runs.

Joyce spent the next season and a half with the Belles. Leo "Red" Murphy, managed through 1949. Unfortunately, the Belles were not a good team. "We called him Pops. He was a fatherly figure to the girls." said Joyce. Injuries slowed Joyce down a little as she appeared in 64 games and managed just 27 hits, 12 RBI and 32 walks.

The 1950 season was the Belles' last in Racine. The franchise moved to Battle Creek, Michigan for the 1951 and 1952 seasons. Joyce was back with the Red Wings for part of 1950 and all of the 1951 season. She got into 70 games with the Belles and Red Wings in 1950 slapping out 50 hits which led to 19 RBI. She also walked 45 times and batted .254. The Red Wings were co-managed by players Mary Carey and Mary Reynolds.

Joyce and Ray got engaged during Christmas week, 1949, so right after the calendar rolled over to 1950 they began to make plans to build their first house in Pleasant Prairie. Joyce knew her playing days were numbered but reported to spring training with the Red Wings. She worked with Ray on the house as long as she could. While she was gone Ray kept working at Nash and on the house. Joyce and Ray got married in Kenosha on December 2, 1950.

The following season, 1951, Joyce Hill, now Joyce Westerman, went back to Peoria for the third and final time in the Red Wings' final season. Under Johnny Rawlings Joyce had another great season batting .242 in a career-high 102 games. She also had career-highs in hits, 86; RBI, 50; and walks, 68. "Johnny Rawlings was really a nice guy." she said. Married life seemed to agree with Joyce as her final two seasons in the league were clearly her best. But Ray was working by himself during the summers of 1951 and 1952 and to Joyce, that didn't seem quite fair. But Ray was supportive 100 percent of Joyce's ball playing and traveled to Joyce's games whenever he could. Ray was a competitive player in the Kenosha city and county leagues and was Joyce's biggest fan. No doubt Joyce found and married the right guy. Not yet 25, Joyce wasn't going to play forever as the league wasn't going to last forever. In 1948 the league had 10 teams and attendance was over 910,000. In 1952 the league was down to six teams and attendance was almost cut in half in 1951.

Joyce and Ray were both working at Nash and making good money. It was a slow process but the couples' first house was coming along. And they managed just fine without having to take out any loans. "We paid for everything. As time went on we bought this and that for the house."said Joyce. "When we were done we owed nothing. I didn't want to get into the situation my parents were in when I was young."

With no home building experience Joyce and Ray took their time and tried to do it right. They built the two-car garage first before actually building the house itself. Ray lived in the garage which had all the amenities of a house. The property was on 88th Avenue near where the Rex Plex is today in Pleasant Prairie. When the house was complete Joyce wasn't sure what their costs were. Asked if she thought her costs were in the neighborhood of $10,000 Joyce shrugged and answered "maybe". They saved a lot of money by doing it themselves. Whereas Uncle George Clausen was there for Cecil and Lillian he was there for Joyce and Ray, too, selling them two acres of the 80-acre family farm.

"At first it was nothing but a gravel pit." Said Joyce. "They were going to put a golf course there." There was no Menard's or Home Depot back then. There were some small hardware stores so Joyce and Ray learned a lot on the fly but got some help from friends and relatives along the way. There was no basement beneath the five-room house. "We were both working." Said Joyce. She worked on the house during the off seasons. "Sometimes we'd work half the night. I'd mix the cement and Ray would pour it." The house finally got finished in the spring of 1955 and just in time as the couple's first daughter, Janet, came into the world on May 25th.

The 1952 Season
Chapter 3

Joyce is going to be mad at me for talking too much about the 1952 season but to me it clearly defines the kind of player Joyce was and is today as a person. She did nothing wrong and deserved every accolade that came her way after what she went through on the field during her first seven years.

2017 is also the 65th anniversary of that tumultuous season. The Kenosha Comets and Peoria Red Wings both closed their doors after the 1951 season so the AAGPBL went into 1952 with six teams. Kenosha posted four winning seasons and four postseason appearances in nine seasons. No championships. But Jean Cione, pitching what amounted to was sidearm in 1950, recorded two no-hitters that season. Peoria had just one winning season, 1948, in six years and Joyce was on that team for awhile. About half of her career was spent playing for either Peoria or Racine. Players from the Comets and Red Wings went into a dispersal draft and divvied up by the remaining six teams. Joyce and Dottie Mueller, a six-foot pitcher/first baseman, were both chosen by South Bend. They were teammates and friends in Peoria. Dottie signed her 1952 contract almost immediately and reported to training camp, while Joyce stayed home in Kenosha unsure as to what she wanted to do. "I was looking forward to working (on the house) next to my husband." She said.

Joyce was coming off a career season in Peoria. She was a good contact hitter and defensive player. Her value was at an all-time high. South Bend manager Karl Winsch doubled as general manager and had full say on personnel matters except when it came to money. He had to be aware of the $5,400 salary cap and thus, player salaries. The Blue Sox sent Joyce a contract in March but she virtually ignored it.

Dr. Harold Dailey, a member of the Blue Sox board of directors, called Joyce after spring training began around May 1 to ask her what she wanted to do. Joyce's answer was she wasn't interested. South Bend had to make it worth her while. Joyce was offered $100 a week but like some veterans around the league she wanted hers tax-free. So Dailey counter-offered her $80 a week plus $30 "under the table" making the total weekly offer $110. "I had to make up my mind." she said. "I wanted to help Ray. I told him if I played I could bank all the money. " The "under the table" money actually came out of the club's "medical expense fund" which was the way around large veteran salaries back then. Perfectly legal as long as the funds didn't dry up. If a sizable claim was made somebody wearing a tie might have to reach into his wallet and pay it. Only $80 a week would count against the team cap, similar to how the signing bonus works in Major League baseball today.

The ownership decided to hold spring training at Playland Park, the Blue Sox's home field, rather than spend money with the rest of the league lodging players somewhere in the south for three weeks. Playland Park was located in a valley next to the St. Joseph River. It has long been torn down and replaced by a golf course and parking lot. The team actually lowered ticket prices in 1952 to $1.50 for box seats, 74 cents for lower grandstand seats and 50 cents for bleacher seats.

With Kenosha and Racine gone by the wayside leaving South Bend and Rockford as the two remaining original franchises in 1952. Actually Racine moved to Battle Creek, Michigan for the franchise's remaining two years. Face it. South Bend and Rockford were able to generate more revenue and were more frugal with their money than the rest of the teams. Otherwise their problem was the same as the other teams in the league: the advent of television. They built good and loyal fan bases and got generous and consistent sponsorship from their communities. The South Bend Tribune and University of Notre Dame were very good to the Blue Sox. Its not that the Comets and Red Wings did a bad job of promoting they simply didn't do enough. Television was the main culprit as people started staying home on summer nights for entertainment. In the AAGPBL South Bend and Rockford turned out to be the business blue prints so it stood to reason why they combined to win six of the league's 12 championships.

So right after Memorial Day, about a week into the regular season, Joyce signed her contract and reported. It took her at least a week to get into playing shape and then was alternated at first base with Mueller. Joyce had missed roughly the first 10 games.

In Peoria in 1951 Joyce collected a career-high 86 hits, 68 walks and 50 RBI. However, the number Winsch liked most was that Joyce struck out just 19 times in 355 official plate appearances. Combine the hits and walks and Joyce was on base over 40 percent of the time. Although Joyce hit just 12 doubles and three triples Winsch saw her as his clean up hitter because she knew how to put the ball in play. "I think I had a pretty good eye up at the plate." she said. "On 3-2 I was looking to swing if the pitch was decent." Mueller started the season at first base and did little pitching since the Blue Sox were deep in that department. She became a spot starter and long reliever.

Joyce, with no spring training, alternated with Mueller at first base until she got up to speed. When Joyce started to hit Mueller went to the bench. And Mueller was not happy about Joyce's arrival. "Dottie and I had been friends in Peoria." said Joyce some years ago. "Maybe she should have been mad at Karl." The Blue Sox manager Karl Winsch, 37 years old that season, was said to be a good baseball man but somewhat abrasive toward his players. In fact, it was written in at least one publication that some of the girls actually tried to avoid him.

Most of the managers in the league were older men who had daughters of their own so they demonstrated more patience and understanding. Winsch was only 12-14 years older than most of the players and treated them more like the older brother toward the kid sister. Winsch had a lot of rules, many of them childish, as he benched, fined or suspended players for any number of things. Most of the girls disliked playing for Winsch, by all accounts, not a players' manager. He grew up in the Philadelphia area and was signed in 1933 as a pitcher by the Phillies. Winsch showed promise, but bounced around the minor leagues for a number of years never making it to "The Show".

Winsch married Jean Haut in 1946. He was working in South Bend after his playing days ended and she was in her first season pitching for the Blue Sox. By 1951 Jean turned into a star pitcher and was popular with her teammates, who knew she was married to Winsch for five years and had a four-year-old boy. Eyebrows were raised in 1951 when Winsch was named Blue Sox manager. Was Jean still going to be one of the girls or was she going to be the manager's wife and informant? Unfortunately, many of the players alienated both of them not wanting to be the subjects of backlash if something got back to either one of them. Joyce turned out to be the voice of reason on the team. She befriended Jean and got along with Karl. Being veterans and the only married girls on the team they had a lot in common. Did Winsch treat his wife differently on the field than the other players? According to a couple of publications the answer was no. It was said he played no favorites. Joyce always went the extra mile to get along with her managers. Plus, Karl coveted Joyce as a player. For the first time in eight years she felt wanted and appreciated. Winsch was a control freak, thus over managed, yet won two championships in four years. "I had a good relationship with Karl." said Joyce. "He was the manager. He was the boss and I was the player. I made some mistakes and he corrected them. I never had a problem with him." Joyce had several things going for her in South Bend. Winsch, having seen her play in Peoria the previous season, saw Joyce as the last piece of the championship puzzle. She was dependable and would be a leader on and off the field.

It was written Winsch was jealous of his wife's success. Jean was one of the best overhand pitchers in the league. Winsch never pitched in a major league game. His wife was not just playing, but dominating, the professional league she pitched in. In four years as South Bend manager Winsch was 232-187 and won the league championships in 1951 and 1952. In the league's final season South Bend lost to Kalamazoo for the league championship. The Blue Sox did not make the playoffs in 1953. Winsch's wife, tired of being caught between her controlling husband and teammates, retired after the 1953 season with her second Player of the Year award. The couple divorced in 1968. Joyce went about her business under Winsch. One time he said she could not ride to a road game with Ray, who came down from Kenosha to watch her play. Another time the couple were house guests of the Winsches during the 1952 season.

Notre Dame football season ticket holders knew Winsch well for over 40 years as he parked and directed cars in the VIP parking lot next to the Athletic and Convocation Center. With Joyce on board the Blue Sox picked up some momentum. They were in first place all the way until mid-August when the wheels started coming off. At the end of the regular season, Sept. 5, South Bend finished three games behind the Jimmie Foxx-led Fort Wayne Daisies meaning the

Blue Sox would have to play the fourth-place Grand Rapids Chicks, managed by Guy Bush, in the first round of the playoffs.

The Blue Sox season hung in the balance about a week before the regular season ended. Their top offensive player, a California girl and All-Star in 1951 named Shorty Pryor, was benched for a poor game the night before. Winsch needed her to pinch run the following night in a late inning of a crucial game. Pryor, thinking she surely would not get into the game, had already taken her spikes off. Winsch, coaching third base, was livid as he glared into the dugout. The result was a week long suspension leading up to the playoffs. The dialogue between the player and Winsch got personal after the game so the player got a month suspension instead of a week thus ending her season. You have to hand it to Winsch, though. He didn't play favorites showing the rest of the team his best offensive player wasn't above his authority. The league stepped in and upheld the suspension just before the playoffs began. A night or two after the incident a team meeting was held. Jean was asked to leave the locker room. What was supposed to be a clear the air meeting turned chippy and physical. Three girls decided to walk off the team if the suspended player wasn't immediately reinstated. Two others followed suit just before the playoffs began. "It was amazing." recalled Joyce. "I remember the fight in the locker room. One girl had to leave and the other five went with her." The thinking amongst the five dissenters was that having made their point everything would blow over and the team would be back at full strength going into the playoffs. After cooler heads prevailed and things settled down in the locker room Joyce spoke up. "Hey we have a game to play tomorrow!" Winsch stuck to his guns and went into the playoffs with nothing close to his best team. Needless to say, Joyce was one of the Dutiful Dozen (named by a newspaper) who chose to stay.

In the semifinal series against Grand Rapids Joyce made a key defensive play at first base forcing a runner out at the plate in the ninth to preserve the win. Game two was much easier as South Bend won 6-1 setting up the championship series with Rockford. The host Peaches won the first game in the best-of-five finals 7-3 but controversy reared its ugly head before the first pitch was thrown in game two. Winsch saw right away the fences had been moved in on Rockford's home field affectionately called "The Peach Orchard". He took a measuring tape and with Blue Sox board member Ernie Longway, a contractor, measured the right field fence to be 188 feet from home plate.

The league rules stated the minimum distance had to be 210 feet. In between games the dimensions of the field were adjusted to make ready for the high school football season. Winsch brought it up at the pre-game meeting at home plate between the managers and umpires. Whereas Winsch protested the shortened distance Rockford manager Bill Allington protested South Bend dressing just 12 players with league rules stipulating 15. Just as game two got under way the league determined 12 was OK as long as the Blue Sox started and finished with at least nine players. One of the defensive players had to be a rookie, thus somebody with less than 50 games of league experience. That too was the rule all season long. Joyce 's ground out to the right side advanced two runners who were doubled in by Faut, but the Peaches, helped by a home run over the shortened right field fence, won the game. Fortunately, South Bend's protest was upheld so game two was replayed. It was Joyce Westerman time in the 12th inning of the replayed game as she scored on Sue Kidd's single. Instead of South Bend being down two games to none the series was tied 1-1.

The next two games were played at South Bend's Playland Field. The Peaches took a 2-1 series lead with a 5-4 win the following night. Joyce's walk off single to right center in the bottom of the 10th lifted South Bend to a 4-3 win tying the series at 2-2. The Peaches had their choice of home field choosing a men's softball park in Freeport, Illinois, about 30 miles from Rockford. With the "Peach Orchard" changed completely over to football the fifth game needed to be played somewhere else. In the winner-take-all game Joyce doubled in the game's first run in the first and with Faut on the mound South Bend won the game and the series 6-3. The local newspaper estimated the crowd to be about 2,000. "Just pure desire." said Joyce. Talk about leadership. Faut won two games and saved another. She also tripled twice, doubled, singled and knocked in five runs in the series. Joyce had four singles, all of them big, two walks and knocked in four runs. That's the stuff MVPs are made of.

The championship celebration dinner was held two nights later in Mishawaka, Indiana, courtesy of the board of directors. Each player and bat girl received a portable radio and carrying case. The largely unpopular Winsch had the last laugh as the "Dutiful Dozen" defied the odds and won a second straight league championship. Once again Joyce was right on about the two decisions she made that season. First, the decision to report and play for the Blue Sox one more season and second, stay and play when five of her teammates chose to walk out. Virtually every key decision in Joyce's life had turned to gold. Joyce Westerman retired a champion in more ways than one. Now she was happy and eager to be Mrs. Ray Westerman full time.

Life After The AAGPBL
Chapter 4

It was a bittersweet time for Joyce in the fall of 1952 when she said good-bye to the game she loved for the man she loved. "I could've played those last two years." she said sadly. Nobody forced her out of the league. Ray never said "quit and stay home". As a competitive player himself in Kenosha Ray supported Joyce all the way. It meant Joyce no longer was going to live the AAGPBL life, especially wear those tacky dresses. "It made me feel sad because I wouldn't need it anymore." she said. When Peoria folded after the 1951 season Joyce hung on to one of her playing tunics which hangs crisp and clean in the closest of her extra bedroom. The league's most die hard fans hoped the league would go on indefinitely but the baseball realists knew its days were numbered. It just could not compete with America's true game, Major League Baseball, once all the stars returned to the diamond. Joyce just knew it was time. Her professional career may have been over and it would be eight years before she played fast pitch again on a Kenosha County diamond. Joyce always got paid on time but was beginning to wonder if that would continue. Every team was having money issues of some kind and paying the girls on time was never a given. Whereas the league spiked in 1948 with 10 teams it was down to five when the league folded after the 1954 season. Even though Joyce may not have gotten the fairest of treatment early on she left the game with no regrets and nothing to be ashamed of. "Except for my family it was the best thing that ever happened to me." she said.

Before you judge her professional numbers too harshly consider that the girls' game came full circle in eight years from fast pitch to baseball. Joyce appeared in 531 games, an average of 66 a season. She totaled 1,515 official plate appearances (not including walks or hit by pitches) and collected 345 hits for a lifetime batting average of .227. The league average for batting average was a hair under .202. Defensively, Joyce's numbers were not bad at all for somebody who caught, played first base and occasionally the outfield. Of the 531 games Joyce appeared in 478 of them were in the field as well as up at the plate. She recorded 2,714 putouts. Now let me explain something.

A catcher was credited with a putout if she hung on to strike three, tagged a runner out at the plate or caught a foul pop up. The catcher was credited with an assist if she threw to one of the bases and the runner was called out. A first baseman received a put out when one of her infielders threw out a batter/runner at first. She also got one for catching a line drive or pop up. The first baseman got an assist if she happened to throw out a runner at one of the other bases. It didn't happen often but it happened. As an outfielder Joyce caught some fly balls for putouts and occasionally threw to a base to nail an overzealous base runner for an assist. Most of you already know the rules of scoring. They are the same as in the men's game but I just want to explain how good Joyce's defensive contributions were. All told Joyce was credited with 208 assists. A third baseman, shortstop or second baseman would get more chances over the course of one season. Joyce averaged an assist about every other game.

Queen of Diamonds

In 478 games in the field Joyce got 3,016 chances meaning she had an opportunity to make a play on the ball that many times. That averages out to just over six chances a game. Joyce took part in 82 double plays and the scenarios would be too numerous to explain. Her lifetime fielding percentage was .969. She made 96 errors in those 3.016 chances. All told she made 97% of the plays that came her way.

If you don't count the first two seasons when Joyce didn't play much that's just 16 errors a season for six full seasons. She made an error about every fourth game. Most full-time infielders don't come close to that although they do handle the ball more. In all due respect to the girls who played in the league errors happened all the time. Even though they were professional players they did not have the range or lateral movement or instincts men did. Plus their hands were soft and small making it difficult to field a hard hit ball right at them. Managers needed to exercise patience. Offensively, Joyce had a great eye at the plate. Except for her first two seasons in which she did not play much Joyce walked more than she struck out by a wide margin, 292-149, almost a 2-1 ratio. If Joyce struck out it was usually swinging. "I had a good eye at the plate." she said. "On 3-2 I was swinging if the pitch was decent." She also swiped 91 bases, not too dusty for somebody who admittedly was not very fast. "I surprised them when I stole a base." she said. For the first time in nine years Joyce lived in Kenosha (1953) the year round. Her time was spent working full time and working on the new house. "That was hard at first." she said. "Especially when it got to be spring training time. "I thought to myself I should be getting ready to play ball. But I was really busy at the time."

A new house was being built and a couple of kids were on the way. Her oldest daughter, Janet, was born on May 25, 1955 and younger daughter, Judy, on December 16, 1957. As fate would have it both girls married first cousins named Vanderford. Today Joyce has a team of her own and then some. Joyce has the two girls, eight grandchildren and three great grandchildren.

Janet never played much competitive softball but spearheaded the AAGPBL reunion in Albuquerque, New Mexico where she lives in 2012. "She was a pretty good hitter." said Joyce. Janet still teaches high school music in Albuquerque. Janet's children are Kier, Tanner, Teagen and Aric and grandchildren Sierra, Ayden and Kier.

Judy played softball and graduated from Carthage College in 1979. She coached Tremper High School's team for one year and still teaches in the Kenosha Unified School District. She is Joyce's helping hand, even when Joyce claimed she didn't need one. Both Janet and Judy graduated from Bradford High School. Judy has four girls – Tracy, Heather, Courtney and Jodi – who were all competitors on the softball diamond and in the pool at Bradford. "They were all great." said former Bradford swim coach Franz Feldmeier. "They were so coachable. Heather was the best athlete in terms of her times. She was very competitive not just in individual events but relays." Heather won a swimming scholarship to Wisconsin-Green Bay and coached the Bradford girls for one season.

Jodi caught and played second base at Wisconsin-Stevens Point. "They all swam and played softball at Bradford" Joyce said proudly. "I'd go to one thing and Ray would go to another." When Joyce showed up at the Bradford pool you could tell grandma was there. "She loved those kids." said Feldmeier. "You can tell she lived for them." Of Judy's four girls the oldest three Tracy (Josh Sunday), Heather (Matt Montey) and Courtney (Nathan Cotter) are married. Jodi is still looking for Mr. Right. No grandchildren yet. Judy is married to Danny Vanderford.

Janet's children are Kier (Josh Lewis), Tanner, Aric and Teagen (Adam Stewart).Joyce's great-grandchildren are Sierra, Ayden and Compton. When Janet and Judy got old enough for school Joyce started working part time at the Woodworth Post Office in Pleasant Prairie under Aunt Esther Clausen, who was the post mistress there.

Joyce transferred into the Kenosha Post Office in 1979 and retired a week into 1986 at age 60. At 34 years old in 1960 "when both my girls were in school" Joyce put the spikes on again. She had been out of the game eight years. "My girls would say, 'Mom, Mom! We never saw you play!'." Joyce said. She had come full circle from playing fast pitch as a teenager, then to baseball and around to fast pitch again as a young adult. Joyce played in Kenosha County leagues and one summer of slow pitch in a Kenosha city league. She pretty much caught and managed a fast pitch team in Milwaukee for a couple of years. Joyce was 59 when she hung up her spikes for good after the 1975 season. Judy graduated from Bradford that spring and played with her mother as much as she could.

The calendar year 1988 was a big year for Joyce. The AAGPBL established a players association (alumni association) for the surviving players in the league. It also got its due from the Baseball Hall of Fame in Cooperstown, New York where a bronze plaque was placed on the wall of the AAGPBL wing. Joyce's name is on it along with almost every young woman who played. Then it was the "League of Their Own" which was filmed partially in Cooperstown. Much of the movie was shot in a small town in down state Indiana. Joyce, like some of the other girls, made non-speaking appearances. Joyce made all but three AAGPBL reunions since they started having them in 1982. She missed the 1991 reunion because the movie was being filmed at the time so Joyce chose the movie. She missed the 2005 reunion in southern California because Ray was too sick to make the trip. The family made it to Albuquerque but turned around and headed home. "He loved going to those reunions." said Joyce. "He was just too sick to go on." "A League Of Their Own", directed by Penny Marshall, gave the almost long forgotten league the visibility and credibility it deserved.

Joyce was far from done in the recognition department. Joyce has taken part in five first pitch ceremonies that she can think of in the last

25 years. She threw out the first pitch before a Milwaukee Brewers' game at old County Stadium. Unfortunately, she does not remember the year. The second time was at the annual reunion in Albuquerque when she was on the field prior to an Isotopes game. She thinks it was 2012. Janet, Joyce's older daughter and Albuquerque resident, did much of the planning and organizing for that reunion. The following year Joyce did not attend because the reunion was held on a cruise ship off of Miami. She just wasn't a cruise person.

On June 6, 2014 Joyce was on the field at Wrigley before the Cubs-Marlins game with nine other ladies who played in the league. She did not actually throw out the first pitch but the footage was played over and over again for the next 12 hours on ESPN's Sportcenter. The last two ceremonies were at Simmons Field in Kenosha. The first was before a Kenosha Twins game somewhere between 1984 and 1992. The second was prior to a Kenosha Kingfish game. Unfortunately, Joyce no longer had the arm. "I had to have Tracy go out there and do it." said Joyce. "I was afraid I wouldn't be able to get the ball up to the plate."

In 2000 Joyce had two open heart surgeries four months apart. She also helped out on the annual AAGPBL reunion at County Stadium that year. Even at 74 years old Joyce refused to back down. In 2003 Joyce, who never played a sport in high school because there weren't any, was inducted into the Kenosha Public School Athletic Hall of Fame receiving the Lifetime Achievement Award. And what a tribute to Joyce. There were no girl's sports in the early forties but she made the Kenosha hall without playing a single sport! Obviously, her recognition came during her time in the AAGPBL. Joyce was also inducted to the Chicago Old-Timers Hall of Fame and Kenosha Old-Timers Hall of Fame.

Joyce's mom and dad and five of her siblings have passed away but perhaps the saddest parting was with Ray. "Judy and I were putting up the Christmas tree the night before when he fell." said

Joyce. Ray had wanted to take a shower but instead went to bed. The following morning on what would have been the couple's 55th wedding anniversary Ray never woke up. He had been suffering from the affects of leukemia. Ray was one heck of a partner and Joyce clearly married the right guy. They both built one house together, worked at Nash together and lived for their girls and grand girls. To this day Joyce still wears her wedding ring. "He played fast pitch. He loved going to the reunions." said Joyce. "He felt worse than I did about missing that reunion (2005) I wanted to be at. He was too sick. We had to turn around and go home."

Back to something positive. Joyce attended the annual AAGPBL reunion August 24-27, 2017 in Cincinnati. Just 116 girls at last count are still with us. Twenty-two made the reunion. Joyce said usually the AAGPBL had a keynote speaker on the first night to welcome the girls and say some nice things. Being in Cincinnati there were a number of possibilities, like a player on the Big Red Machine from the 1970's. There were no players this time. Just Pete Rose's first ex-wife, Karolyn. Pete, of course, is still under a lifetime ban from baseball for betting on sports, particularly his own Cincinnati Reds. With the AAGPBL a part of Major League Baseball and the Hall of Fame Pete was not invited. Joyce said Karolyn owns a bar in Cincy and invited the girls over for cocktails. The girls were recognized on the field Thursday night during the Cubs-Reds game. On Saturday they signed autographs for fans for what was supposed to be an hour and a half. It was more like two hours, said Joyce. "Boy, were we tired when we finally got done." There was memorabilia and sportswear that was sold. And once again Joyce Westerman continued to live her dream.

A League Of Big Names
Chapter 5

The 1992 movie "A League of Their Own" gave the long-forgotten All-American Girls Professional Baseball League a ton of credibility and recognition. So did a number of men and women who either managed or played in it.

Bill Wambsganss

The stocky little Wambsganss played in the major leagues between 1914 and 1926. He was the every day second baseman for the Cleveland Naps/Indians for 10 seasons and also played for the Boston Red Sox and Philadelphia Athletics. While playing in the 1920 World Series, won by the Indians, "Wamby" pulled off an unassisted triple play in game 5 that is still the only unassisted triple play in World Series history. Hall of Famer **Tris Speaker** was the star center fielder and manager of the Tribe.

Twenty-year-old Joyce Hill was dealt to the Fort Wayne Daisies, which Wambsganss managed, from the South Bend Blue Sox for the final three weeks of the 1946 season. Joyce does not recall anything significant about playing for him, although he rarely looked her way on the bench. "He was a nice guy." she said.

Max Carey

The Baseball Hall of Famer chose baseball over the pulpit and went on to play 20 years mostly with the Pittsburgh Pirates. The speedy centerfielder, once a high school track star, stole 738 bases placing him ninth on Major League Baseball's all-time stolen base list. Carey finished his career with the Brooklyn Dodgers and managed them in 1931 and 1932. Carey managed the Milwaukee Chicks to the AAGPBL championship in their first and only season in Milwaukee in 1944. For the next 10 seasons the Chicks played in Grand Rapids, Michigan. Carey was league president between 1945 and 1949 and returned to the dugout to manage the Fort Wayne Daisies in 1950 and 1951. Like many big leaguers Carey had a number of investments, in this case real estate, that went belly up after the 1929 stock market crash. He wrote and contributed to two baseball magazines and was once the Florida state racing commissioner. Carey, along with Dave Bancroft, were the only two men to manage in both the AAGPBL and major leagues.

Jimmie Foxx

The man baseball writers referred to as "Double X" and "The Beast" Jimmie Foxx socked 534 homers in a 20-year career as a first baseman mostly with the Philadelphia Athletics and Boston Red Sox. By the time "Double X" hung up his spikes he was baseball's all-time leader in home runs by a right handed batter. Babe Ruth, a left handed swinger, retired as the overall leader with 714. Foxx hit his 500th homer for Boston on September 24, 1940 at age 32 years, 336 days. Nobody younger hit their 500th homer until Alex Rodriguez hit his on August 4, 2007 for the Yankees at age 32 years, eight days, an almost 67-year gap.

Foxx managed just one year in the AAGPBL that being with the Fort Wayne Daisies in 1952. Joyce played against Foxx's Daisies during that regular season. One source wrote the Hall of Famer quit after one season because he was sick of the long bus trips. On one of the Daisies' visits to South Bend the 45-year-old Foxx treated the crowd to a long ball hitting exhibition Joyce still talks about today. Keep in mind that Playland Field, home of the Blue Sox, was much smaller than any minor or major league park. "It was incredible." Joyce said. "Most of the girls never saw a major leaguer before. Their mouths dropped when he hit one after another over the fence, over the lights, over the trees, over everything." Life after baseball was not very good to "Double X". He lost a ton of money in the stock market crash and had a history of heart problems. He started to lose his sight toward the end of his career due to a beaning he got. Unfortunately, he drank too much. While dining with his brother in Miami Foxx choked on a piece of meat and died a couple of weeks later short of his 60th birthday. His second wife died in the same manner less than one year earlier.

Bill Allington

There is no doubt Bill Allington was the AAGPBL's best and most successful manager. Allington went 583-398 in nine seasons leading the Rockford Peaches to six playoff appearances in seven years winning four championships. The Fort Wayne Daisies made the playoffs both years he managed them His teams won more games than they lost in all nine of his seasons. Joyce never played for Allington but played against his teams many times. "He was a good teacher." Joyce said. "He was tough on his girls, though."

Allington's methods were effective as he batted .327 in 1,145 career minor league games. He never made the major leagues even though he had some incredible minor league seasons. He was a career baseball man on and off the field. When the league folded following the 1954 season Allington organized a traveling team of former AAGPBL players that barnstormed the country for three years. Many of their opponents were men's teams and they did not like losing to women.

Guy Bush

The Mississippi Mudcat managed the Battle Creek Belles, who used to be the Racine Belles, to a 30-80 mark in 1951 and a 43-67 finish in 1952 when the Belles lost their three-game playoff series to Joyce's Blue Sox. Overall, Bush had a respectable major league career going 176-136 in 23 seasons. His best stint was with the Cubs for whom he went 152-101 primarily as a starter in 12 seasons.

While pitching for the Pirates Bush secured his place in baseball history. On May 25, 1935 he served up home runs Nos. 713 and 714 to Babe Ruth, who was playing out his career with the Boston Braves. Even though the Babe was washed up by then he had a career day collecting four hits, three of them home runs, and six RBI. Bush, a southerner from Mississippi, literally hated the flamboyant Ruth, a Baltimore native, in a rivalry dating back to the Cubs-Yankees World Series in 1932. But the Babe had the last laugh on that day hitting his final home run over the roof at old Forbes Field in Pittsburgh.

Dave Bancroft

Between 1915 and 1930 "Beauty" was considered by a number of sportswriters to be one of the best shortstops of his time. He always called his pitchers "Beauty" when they threw a pitch leading directly to an out. As a rookie in 1915 Bancroft and veteran pitcher **Grover Cleveland Alexander** led the Philadelphia Phillies to their first National League pennant. The Phillies lost to the **Babe Ruth/Tris Speaker**-led Red Sox four games to one in the World Series.

Bancroft went on to play on three more NL pennant winners

including the 1922 and 1923 World Series champion New York Giants. There he played for John McGraw, perhaps the greatest manager at that time. Bancroft was dealt to the Boston Braves in a multi-player trade that included Casey Stengel after the 1923 season. Between 1924 and 1927 the future Hall of Famer was player-manager of the Braves but never won more than 70 games in any one season.

Bancroft and Max Carey were the only two men to manage in both the AAGPBL and major leagues. "Beauty" had one good season out of the three and a half he managed in the AAGPBL guiding the Blue Sox to a 75-46 record in 1949 but lost to the Rockford Peaches for the league championship.

The Iowa-born Bancroft, who lived and died in Superior, Wisconsin, was 55-55 as Blue Sox skipper in 1950 and replaced by Karl Winsch the following season. "Beauty" went 11-46 in the first half of 1951 with the Battle Creek Belles and replaced by Bush. He also managed the Chicago Colleens developmental traveling team in 1948. Joyce played against Bancroft's teams many times.

Yes, Women Can Play This Game
Chapter 6

Kathryn "Dr. Kate" Vondereau

Like Joyce "Dr. Kate" caught for eight seasons in the AAGPBL. The reason I mention her now is she is one of the most successful AAGPBL alumni. Dr. Kate, who never married, saved her money and went back to school during the off seasons earning her Bachelors and Masters degrees at the University of Indiana and doctorate at the University of Iowa.

The Indiana native spent most of her teaching life as a coach, physical education instructor and administrator at the University of Wisconsin-Whitewater where she was the school's first softball coach. Dr. Kate was inducted into the Warhawk Hall of Fame in 1996 and of course, is on the AAGPBL plaque in Baseball's Hall of Fame. This writer took two coaching classes from Dr. Kate. I believe they were volleyball and coaching principles in 1976. Dr. Kate is a wonderful person and I wish I could have taken all of my English and Journalism courses with her. I had no idea she was an AAGPBL player until many years later when Joyce told me she was traded for Dr. Kate once. I last saw Dr. Kate at the AAGPBL reunion in Milwaukee in 2000. Since then I am told she lost her eyesight and lives in Sumner, Washington. She turned 90 on September 27, 2017.

Toni Palermo

The scholarly Toni didn't play much but is another highly successful alumnus. The Forest Park, Illinois native played parts of the 1949 and 1950 seasons with the Chicago Colleens and Springfield Sallies, both developmental traveling teams. Toni went to spring training with Joyce's Blue Sox in 1952 but did not make the team. After her time in the AAGPBL ended the former shortstop majored in history, math and English at Alverno College in Milwaukee, earned three Masters degrees and her doctorate at the University of Wisconsin-Madison, where she also taught social work. Toni is long retired but still serves as Vice President on the AAGPBL, Inc. Board of Directors. "You wouldn't believe all the dairies she kept." said Joyce. Well believe this! On top of her many academic achievements Sister Toni found time to become a nun!

Joan Holderness

Kenosha-born Joan began her career as a batgirl with the Comets in 1947. Her mother was strict and kept Joan's softball involvement to a minimum. Her father was a bit more understanding so he drove her down to a tryout camp where she made the cut and signed by the Comets for the 1949 and part of the 1950 seasons. Joan played half of 1950 and half of the 1951 seasons with the Grand Rapids Chicks and finished up her career with the Battle Creek Belles in 1951. Joan was a utility player playing everywhere except pitcher and catcher. She had 43 hits in 119 career games.

Joan's dream was to play for her hometown Comets and she did just that. Upon moving to Florida after her mother passed away Joan discovered bowling to be her new found love. She was inducted into three Florida bowling hall of fames by the time she was 70. I found no information as to how Joan made her living in Florida or whether or not she married and had a family of her own. Joan passed away on July 6, 2017 in Spring Hill, Florida.

Kenosha's Darlene "Mickey" Mickelsen, Barbara Galdonik and Donna Becker

All three Kenosha-born ladies played in the league for less than two seasons each. "Mickey" was the fourth outfielder on the original Kenosha Comets in 1943. She got into 47 games as the Comets finished last in the inaugural four-team league at 43-65. Mickey will always be known for her sixth inning single that gave the Comets their first ever victory over Racine 7-6 at Lakefront Stadium. The game was played on May 30, 1943 before a crowd of about 600 under threatening skies. Mickey did not play in 1944 but got into three games with South Bend in 1945 going 1-for-4 and then "dropped out of sight", according to the AAGPBL website.

She batted an even .200 in 50 career games (33-for-165), walked 10 times and knocked in 29 runs. Mickey passed away in August, 1969. Barb played third base for the Comets in 1950 and the Battle Creek Belles in 1951. Statistics for Barb were unavailable. She passed away in Superior, Wisconsin in August, 2003.

Donna, who turned 85 on August 6, 2017, taught school in Kenosha and Racine for many years. She pitched for the Kalamazoo Lassies in 1951 but her statistics were unavailable.

Dottie Schroeder

Dottie was the Cal Ripken, Jr. of the league as she was the only player to play all 12 seasons. It is not known if she played in every single game but appeared in 1,249 games, an average of 104 a season, and totaled 870 hits, second most in league history. The pigtailed Dottie was a bundle of energy and favorite among teammates, opponents and fans. As one writer put it "Nobody signed more autographs than Dottie."

The farm girl from the Champaign, Illinois area played her first game at 15 years, two and a half months old, the second youngest ever to play in the AAGPBL. The three-time All-Star led all shortstops in fielding as a rookie. Dottie was a career .211 hitter smacking 42 home runs, 36 of them in her latter six seasons as she grew older and stronger. Dottie, who had a twin brother Don, played her first two and a half seasons in South Bend, the next two and a half in Kenosha and the next five in Fort Wayne. She played her final two seasons with the Kalamazoo Lassies as she went out a league champion in 1954. "She was something, boy." said Joyce. After her AAGPBL time ended Dottie played three years with the Bill Allington Traveling All-Stars playing a barnstorming schedule against many men's teams holding their own and often beating many of them. Dottie, who never married, passed away in December, 1996 of a brain aneurysm.

Jean Faut

When the question comes up who was the league's greatest pitcher **Jean Faut** is definitely in the conversation. With Jean throwing strikes and Joyce clutch-hitting the two veterans led the Blue Sox to the league championship in 1952. Hard to argue with Jean's numbers as she pitched both sidearm and then overhand during her eight seasons. She did not pitch softball style when she entered the league in 1946 and left after the 1953 season with a 140-64 record and a microscopic 1.23 earned run average in 230 pitching appearances. She pitched four no-hitters, two of them perfect games, and was Player of the Year in 1951 and 1953.

Jean, who married Blue Sox manager **Karl Winsch** in 1946, accomplished most of her success trying to be mother, teammate, player and wife to the manager. Jean won four games and saved one in South Bend's 1952 playoff run and added two timely triples and a double at the plate. She either played third base or pinch hit when she wasn't pitching. Jean, tired of being caught between her teammates and over managing husband, retired after the 1953 season. She said in her biography she wished she would have pitched in the league's final season, 1954. Jean pitched all eight seasons in South Bend winning league championships in 1951 and 1952. In terms of longevity of service to one team Jean is tied for second with eight consecutive years. A great athlete, Jean bowled her way on to the Woman's Professional Bowling Tour and became a scratch golfer. The 92-year-old Jean, a native of East Greenville, Pennsylvania, now lives in Rock Hill, South Carolina.

If You Like Numbers Here's Some More
Chapter 7

As of September 1, 2017 **Mary Pratt,** who turns 99 on November 30, 2017, is the oldest living AAGPBL player. **Dorice Reid, Charlotte Smith, Lillian Lukey** and **Gladys Davis** have or will turn 98 in 2017. **Mary Holda-Elrod**, who was an original South Bend Blue Sock in 1943, died in Utica, Ohio in 2016 at age 100. She was the league's only centurion.

Maxine Drinkwater-Simmons is the youngest surviving league member at 81, months ahead of **Mary Lou Graham**, who began her brief two-year career as the South Bend batgirl. Nine girls have or will turn 82 in 2017.

Madeline English and Margaret Wenzel both played all nine of their seasons with the Racine/Battle Creek Bells. English once stole seven bases in one game.

Jean Faut (South Bend) and **Edythe Perlick** (Racine) played all eight of their seasons with one team.

On June 5, 1952 **Dolly Vanderslip** played in her first AAGPBL game at 15 years, one day. **Dottie Schroeder** is next having played her first game at 15 years, two and a half months.

Faut, Connie Wisniewski and Helen Nicol hold almost all of the pitching records. Faut's 1.23 earned run average is the absolute lowest. Wisniewski's ERA was 1.48 but nosed out Faut for winning percentage, .690 to 6.86, going 107-48. Nicol had the most wins, 163; losses, 118; and strikeouts, 1,076.

Faut has two perfect games to her credit, **Annabelle Lee, Doris Sams and Carolyn Morris one each.** Annabelle certainly deserves the Tough Luck Award if the league had one. She also threw a second no-hitter but finished her career 63-96 with a stingy ERA of 2.25. There is no nice way to say it. Annabelle pitched on some bad teams.

In terms of offense Schroeder holds six records. She played the most seasons, 12; most games, 1,249; RBI, 431; walks, 696; at-bats, 4,129; and strikeouts, 566. She is second in hits with 870.

Dorothy Kamenshek had the most hits, 1,090; and total bases, 1,300.

Eleanor Callow is the home run queen with 55; triples, 60; and slugging percentage, .549.

Ten-year veteran **Sophie Kurys** was **the Rickey Henderson** of the league with 1,114 stolen bases and runs leader with 688. In 1946 she stole 201 bases. Seven Cuban-born girls played in the league. The league trained in Cuba in 1947 and the crowds were said to be bigger than the Brooklyn Dodgers attracted when they trained there. And they had an attraction of their own in **Jackie Robinson.** Back then before **Fidel Castro** came into power (1959) Cubans could come and go as they pleased as long as they had the means to do so. It is not known how many Cuban girls were invited to try out for the league or specifically how they got to the United States but they did. A couple of final notes.

A total of 640 girls once occupied roster spots in the league's 12 seasons. Fifty-seven of them were Canadians. Michigan was tops in the United States with 34. There were 25 Long Island, New Yorkers, three Greeks and two Jewish girls. Fourteen girls were Wisconsin-born. A total of 23 states were represented. One of the Greek girls, **Anastasia Patikis**, was a native of Kaukauna, Wisconsin but her parents were both born and raised in Greece. Anastasia was a long time resident of Racine and one of Joyce's dearest friends in the league. She passed away on March 12, 2016 three days before her 90th birthday.

Managers
Chapter 8

Kenosha Comets managers

John "Josh" Billings was the Comets' first manager in 1943 leading them to a 56-52 slate in the league's first year before losing a playoff series to the Racine Belles. Billings was primarily a backup catcher in 11 seasons with the Cleveland Naps, who became the Cleveland Indians in 1920, St. Louis Browns and Detroit Tigers. He batted .217 with 29 RBI in 243 career games. As a member of the 1920 Indians Billings was a World Series champion and teammates with **Tris Speaker** and **Bill Wambsganss**, another AAGPBL manager.

It was written Billings' 1943 salary was $100 a week.

Marty McManus was a major league infielder playing in 1,652 games with the Browns, Tigers, Red Sox and Braves. He was a career .289 hitter scoring 1,008 runs and batting .300 or better four times. McManus led the Comets to a 62-54 season in 1944 and then lost to the Milwaukee Chicks in the championship series.

Eddie Stumpf was a catcher by trade who according to his

Wikipedia bio, "never tasted major league action". He was a career baseball man playing, coaching, managing, scouting and working in the front offices of minor league and independent league teams. "Stumpy" failed to inspire the Comets in 1945 finishing last in the now eight-team league at 41-69.

Press Cruthers did not fair much better in 1946 finishing seventh out of eight teams at 42-70. Cruthers played parts of the 1913 and 1914 seasons with the Connie Mack-led Philadelphia Athletics managing just six big league hits. He was on the A's World Series roster in 1913.

Cruthers took a liking to Kenosha deciding to make it his home in Pleasant Prairie until his death in 1976.

Ralph Shinners, who Wikipedia says is Marquette University's only major league player, was a center fielder by trade batting .300 or better in seven of his nine minor league seasons. Shinners played parts of five seasons in the big leagues. He was on the roster of the 1922 and 1923 World Series champion New York Giants. His best season was his last with the St. Louis Cardinals in 1925 batting .295 with seven homers and 36 RBI in 74 games. Shinners was a hitting machine in the minors collecting 1,214 hits in 1,152 games. Unfortunately, Shinners' hitting ability didn't rub off on the Comets who finished last in 1947 at 43-69.

Chet Grant and Johnny Gottselig were the two highest profile managers to manage in Kenosha. Not only was Grant a three-sport player at Notre Dame he was the 18-year-old sports editor of the South Bend Tribune in 1910. After Grant put in some time with Uncle Sam he enrolled at Notre Dame at age 28 and quarterbacked for Knute Rockne in 1920 and 1921. He also returned a punt 95 yards for a touchdown, an Irish record at the time.

One of Grant's teammates in 1920 was a terminally ill George Gipp. Grant returned to complete his final two seasons of eligibility. Later he accepted an offer to coach the backfield under Elmer Layden, one of Notre Dame's legendary Four Horsemen, between 1934 and

1940. He did so-so as Comets' manager finishing 61-64 and in fourth place in the five-team Western Division in 1948. Kenosha lost its playoff series to the Belles three games to none. In Grant's second season the 1949 Comets finished a respectable 58-55 good for fourth among the eight teams, but missed the championship round of the playoffs.

Like Grant, Gottselig wasn't a pure baseball man but knew how to win having played a winger on two Stanley Cup championship teams (1934, 1938) with the Chicago Blackhawks. Gottselig also picked up another ring in 1961 as an executive in the Blackhawks' front office. The Comets enjoyed their best season record wise in 1950 going 64-46 but lost three games to one to Rockford in the playoffs.

The final curtain fell on the Comets in 1951 as they went out with a franchise worst 36-65 record under player-manager **Ernestine "Teeny" Petras**. It was rumored prior to the 1951 season that it would likely be the Comets' last so the brain trust didn't bother hiring an experienced manager. The acrobatic Petras was a proven player and said to be the Ozzie Smith of her day. The strong armed shortstop led the league in fielding four times and sported a career fielding percentage of .943. As a slap-hitting lead-off batter Petras was a weapon collecting 552 career hits, 342 walks and stealing 420 bases. Up until a few years ago Petras, who turned 92 on October 22, 2017, was working in support capacities for women's organizations in her native Barnegat, New Jersey.

Managers Joyce played for

Joyce's first manager in the league was **Benny Meyer** in 1945. The 19 and a half year old Joyce got off on the wrong foot with the hot-headed Meyer who kept her on the Grand Rapids Chicks bench most of the season. "Aahh! He was OK, I guess." said Joyce. "When I first got there he embarrassed me in front of everybody because I didn't know all the league rules." Meyer's temper was the subject of a

1929 newspaper article when he was a coach with the Detroit Tigers. "Loud" was perhaps the nicest compliment he got in that article.

Meyer, an outfielder, played parts of four seasons with the Phillies and Dodgers and batted a respectable .265 in 310 big league games. Joyce looked like she was going to be the Comets' opening day catcher in 1946 but was traded instead to South Bend where she played little under Grant. Joyce was traded to the affable **Wambsganss**' Fort Wayne Daisies team with about three weeks left in the season. It was on to Peoria in 1947 where **Gottselig** finally gave Joyce a chance to play.

Leo Schrall took over the following year and led the Red Wings to a 71-55 record, clearly the franchise's high water mark in six seasons. Joyce was traded again, this time to Racine, before the Red Wings were swept in three games in the playoffs.

Leo (Red) Murphy had a nice run in Racine leading the Belles to three straight playoff appearances including a league championship in 1946. Joyce played most of 1948 and all of 1949 for Murphy. "A lot of the girls called him Pops." Joyce said. "He was a fatherly figure to many of them." At least she got to sleep in her own bed in Pleasant Prairie. It was back to Peoria for Joyce in 1950 and 1951. **Mary Carey and Mary Reynolds** were players and co-managers of the team in 1950 that finished a dismal 44-63-2.

Joyce had her best season statistically under **Johnny Rawlings** in 1951, who played on three pennant winning teams Giants 1922, 1923 and Pirates (1925). He basically spent his 13-year career bouncing back and forth between the minors and majors. Rawlings led six AAPGBL teams in his eight seasons to the playoffs winning the championship with the Chicks in 1947. "He was a good guy." said Joyce. Joyce's final season in South Bend in 1952 was one for the tabloids.

Karl Winsch, who toiled as a pitcher in the Phillies organization, was the manager. The uncharismatic, yet successful Winsch, managed four seasons guiding the Blue Sox to league championships in 1951 and 1952. It helped considerably that Winsch was married to one of the league's top pitchers in **Jean Faut**. And even though Faut was caught between her controlling husband and teammates she was Player of the Year in 1951 and 1953. Faut stepped away from the game after that 1953 season. Once Joyce signed her 1952 contract and reported to the Blue Sox the smartest move Winsch probably made was inserting her into the starting lineup at first base.

As long as we're on the subject of managers....

Eddie Ainsmith (Rockford, 1947) was the only AAGPBL manager to play with **Ty Cobb** in Detroit between 1919 and 1921. **Bill Rodgers** (Peoria, 1946) was the only manager to play with **Babe Ruth** in the 1915 World Series season as a member of the Red Sox. He also played with another Hall of Famer in **Tris Speaker**. Bancroft, a rookie, and **Bert Niehoff** (South Bend, 1943, 1944) was the double play combination at short and second for the 1915 Phillies in their World Series loss to the **Babe Ruth**-led Red Sox.

The 1926 season was the last for Cobb as player/manager in Detroit. **Josh Billings** and **Marty McManus**, Kenosha's first two managers, were both listed on the 1927 Tigers roster, a year after the "Georgia Peach" left the team. McManus, who was said to love betting the horses as much as he loved playing baseball, also played for the 1934 Boston Braves. The Babe assumed McManus' roster spot in 1935 and finished out his career by the time that season was two months old.

Len Zintac (Chicago, 1949, Springfield, 1950) was the league's oldest manager passing away at 95 in 2015. Not much is known about **Joe Cooper** (Battle Creek, 1952 and Muskegon, 1953) only that he is the AAGPBL's oldest living manager turning 94 on July 30, 2017. **Charley Stis** (Racine 1945) passed away at 94, Grant at 93.

More History
Chapter 9

Ann Hartnett, no apparent relation to Gabby, was the first girl signed to play in the league in 1943 as a Comet. Hartnett was primarily a catcher but also played some third base. Hartnett and Phillip Wrigley's wife Helen designed the uniforms the girls wore all 12 seasons. Hartnett played five seasons, four in Kenosha and the last one in Peoria. After the 1947 season Hartnett left the game to become a nun, a promise she made to her dying mother.

Annabelle Lee pitched the league's first perfect game. She is the aunt of lefthander **Bill "Spaceman" Lee**, who had some big seasons pitching for Boston and Montreal. **Helen Callaghan** is the mother of **Casey Candaele**, an infielder who played for three major league teams during the eighties and nineties. **Doris Sams** and **Jean Faut**, a teammate and friend of Joyce's on the 1952 champion Blue Sox, were the only two players to be named Player of the Year twice. Sams was named in 1947 and 1949, Faut in 1951 and 1953 leaving the game after that season.

Betty Foss had league bests in doubles, 34; and triples, 17; in 1952. In 1953 she had a league season high 144 hits. **Joanne Weaver** hit 29 home runs and finished with 254 total bases in the league's final season, 1954.

Kenosha's professional athletes

Alan "the Horse" Ameche, NFL
Dick Bosman, MLB
Jim Barnhill, former AFL referee
Bob "Gabby" Hartmann, MLB
Ray Berres, MLB
Tom Bienemann, NFL
Joyce Hill-Westerman, AAGPBL
Donna Becker, AAGPBL
Darlene Mickelsen, AAGPBL
Barbara Galdonik, AAGPBL
Tom Braatz, NFL
Frankie Conley, Boxing
Fritz Cronin, NFL
Press Cruthers, MLB
Paul Russo, auto racing
James Hipp Vaughn, MLB
Nate Mikolas, minor league BB
Augie Schmidt, minor league BB
Tom Barndollar
Tre Waynes, NFL
Melvin Gordon, NFL
Nick Van Exel, NBA
Ben Dyer, MLB
Gene Englund, NBA
Harvey Green, MLB
Jack Hammond, MLB
Ken Huxhold, NFL
Chet Kozel, NFL
Gavin Lux, Minor League BB
Ollie O'Mara, MLB
Charlie Pechous, MLB
Phil Pettey, NFL
Elmer Rhenstrom, NFL,
Ralph Thomas, NFL
Bobby Zeihen, minor league BB
Randy Gentile, minor league BB
Joan Holderness, AAGPBL

As long as I'm giving some love to Kenosha's professionals I'm going to include the Kenosha Maroons of the National Football League. Yes, you read this right. Back in 1924 Kenosha was in the NFL! Eat your hearts out! Unfortunately, the glory lasted five games as the Maroons, strapped for money, talent and probably coaching, folded at 0-4-1.

The Green Bay Packers were drawing about 5,000 fans a game back then. Kenosha's only home game ended in a 6-6 tie with the Hammond Pros. One source listed the attendance at 600, another at

800. That game took place at the Nash Employees Athletic Field on the corner of 52nd Street and 29th Avenue. Back then Nash was Kenosha's premier athletic field for football, baseball and softball. It also had tennis courts and a playground for Nash employees and their families. The field was first used in 1923. The Maroons were purchased the following year from Toledo, Ohio investors by the City of Kenosha. Nash and the Simmons Bedding Company were key supporters. Somewhere in the early 1940s the Nash Field was replaced by an extension of the main factory which began the assembly of airplane engine parts. Joyce worked with the airplane engines off and on upon graduating from high school in 1943.

Lakefront Stadium, which sat where the marina is today on Kenosha's lakefront, was the Comets' home between 1943 and 1947. Lakefront, according to Kenosha History Center records, was first used in 1937 and probably constructed in 1936 or earlier. Joe Louis trained there for his June 22, 1937 World Heavyweight Boxing Championship fight against James J. Braddock. Louis won the bout, held in Chicago, and went on to hold the belt for 140 months or almost 12 years.

Joyce remembers having to walk the four blocks from Kenosha High School to Lakefront for gym class. So did everybody else who went to Kenosha High School/Bradford through the end of the 1979-80 school year. The new Bradford opened in the fall, 1980 on the corner of Washington Road and 39th Avenue. Finally, the Red Devils' own stadium just north of the school opened in the fall of 2016. The Comets played on a makeshift diamond at the southwest end of the field. City league slow pitch leagues played there, too. It was an easy home run into the right field bleachers. Weather played a key role in keeping attendance down as rain, wind, cold and fog were unwanted guests at Lakefront. Some of the Comets complained they could not see their centerfielder on foggy occasions. Lakefront was primarily a football field surrounded by a cinder track. It was home to high school and junior high football plus track and field meets for years. Lakefront was the home field for the Kenosha Cardinals semi-pro football team for five years.

On September 9, 1940 the Cards hosted the Green Bay Packers, led by 37-year-old Johnny "Blood" McNally and 31-year-old Beattie Feathers. On a balmy late summer evening with a breeze blowing in off Lake Michigan the Pack prevailed over the Cards 17-0. The Packers returned in November, 1941 to steamroll the Kenosha team 65-2.

Also in 1941, the Cardinals lost to the Chicago Bears 27-6; the Philadelphia Eagles 35-6; tied the Chicago Cardinals 21-21; and lost to the Cleveland Rams 34-0. It was home to the 1950 Kenosha High School team which at the time was considered the greatest high school football team in state history. Alan Ameche, the Heisman Trophy winner-to-be at Wisconsin and future Baltimore Colt, was clearly Kenosha's best player.

Lakefront's final hoorah was the 1975-76 school year. All three city high school football teams shifted to brand new Anderson Field the following year. Lakefront was torn down in 1980 making way for the Kenosha marina. If the AAGPBL was a league of its own **Simmons Field** is certainly a field of its own. Among the countless teams that called Simmons home since 1920 were the Comets who played their final four seasons there between 1948 and 1951. Simmons Field was once the property of the Simmons Bedding Company which built the stadium for its baseball team. It has been the property of the City of Kenosha for years. At one time Simmons Field was promoted as the oldest minor league baseball park in America while the Kenosha Twins played there between 1984 and 1992. It would be a huge undertaking but one could write a book about the 97-year-old history of Simmons Field. And just as it did at Lakefront Lake Michigan weather played a huge part in poor attendance even though Simmons was roughly eight blocks from the lake. Bob Feller, Warren Spahn, Satchel Paige and

Rick Sutcliffe all pitched there. Sutcliffe made a rehab appearance for the Peoria Chiefs against the Twins before a paid crowd of 4,387 spectators in July, 1991. Today Simmons Field never looked better and has been the home of the Kenosha Kingfish of the Northwoods League since 2014.

Some of the many events Simmons Field hosted over the years were the Optimist Little League All-Star Game, City Slowpitch Tournament, NCAA baseball regionals hosted by Carthage College, Jaycee and Kiwanis Junior Leagues and junior high football, which was like playing in quick sand when it rained. Also, the Kenosha Pirates, Kings, Chiefs and Kroakers played there just to name a few teams.

How It All Began
Chapter 10

Phillip K. Wrigley, Branch Rickey and Paul V. Harper were dead serious about putting a quality product on the field when they founded the All-American Girls Professional Baseball League in 1943. They wanted women who could play at a high level. They also wanted their players to act like ladies on and off the field. Minor league baseball took the biggest hit going from 41 teams in 1941 to nine less than two years later. With many of the stars overseas the major league clubs filled their rosters with minor leaguers. The girls would be playing for the good 'ole boys and doing things their way.
A men's game and a men's business. This was going to be professionally run and professionally played baseball. The game wasn't going to be a spinoff of pro wrestling or roller derby or some soap opera. It definitely wasn't going to take on a tavern league atmosphere. Lady-like celebrations were OK but the league would have no part of the chest thumping, forearm bumping and knuckle crunching we see today. No tattoos, no performance enhancing drugs as if there were any back then.

Image was everything. The three investors hired scouts from all walks of sports to scour America and southern Canada for fast pitch talent. That's how serious they were about making this thing work. They even selectively placed ads in some of the country's largest newspapers in hopes of finding diamonds in the rough. **Ken Sells,** a Wrigley employee, was the league's first president. Hall of Famer **Max Carey** took over in 1945 after leading the Milwaukee Chicks to the championship the previous year. They were not sure a lot of money, if any, would be made off this venture. The long term goal was to keep the game in America's minds and hearts while World War II and then the Korean Conflict played themselves out. It was anybody's guess how long the wars would last thus nobody knew how long the new league would last.

Failure wasn't really an option since most of baseball's best players were stationed overseas. It was America's game and the three investors needed the ladies to make an impact. Their job was to look good and give the paying customers good baseball. On the bright side this would give the girls an opportunity to show America they could be professional ballplayers and be good at it. They also had the opportunity to make some money, more than most of them could be making at their hometown jobs. That and keeping up the country's morale.

In 1942 the United States' involvement in World War II was less than a year old. If the three original investors were going to make a move it better be soon. So they decided then to assume a conservative approach. They began with four franchises—Kenosha, Racine, South Bend and Rockford—all within an hour and a half drive of Chicago.

Wrigley invested $100,000 to get things started. $18,500 went to each of the four teams. The remaining $10,000 went to start the league office in Chicago.

The game, at least to start with, would be fast pitch, something the girls were more familiar playing. The pitching rubber was 40 feet from home plate and flat as opposed to being on a mound. The bases were 65 feet apart. The designated hitter rule was 30 years off into the distance. Replay was unimaginable since games were not televised but covered conservatively in the local newspapers and occasionally on radio. During the first three years of the league's existence, while Wrigley was the principle owner, it would be called the All-American Girls Softball League.

Arthur Meyerhoff, an advertising executive, bought out Wrigley's interests after the 1945 season and called the league the All-American Girls Professional Baseball League. The game slowly transcended from fast pitch to baseball but it wasn't true baseball yet. By 1948 the pitching rubber was put back to 50 feet and bases to 75 feet. The ball shrunk from 12 inches circumference to 10 inches to 9 3/8 inches. The pitching motion was sidearm or three quarters. Interest in the league spiked in 1948. There were 10 teams and league attendance topped the 910,000 mark. The entire league trained in Havana, Cuba prior to the 1947 and 1948 seasons.

Helen Wrigley and **Ann Hartnett**, who was the first player signed by the league, designed the uniform. It resembled a combination of figure skating, field hockey and tennis outfit. It was called a "tunic made of a heavy twill for a rugged endurance." Each player was issued a home and road uniform. The road uniform was usually a lighter color. The girls were also issued a baseball style hat, wide belt and matching pairs of bloomers and socks. A circular patch with the name of the team was sewn on the sternum area.

Joyce told me the uniform "took some time to get used to" as they weren't built for comfort especially in hot, humid weather. One could appreciate the owners' efforts to make the girls look more like ladies on the field. One would have to wonder, though, if the quality of play would have been enhanced if the girls were outfitted more comfortably, say in shorts or a soft cotton knicker like men. The footwear was steel spikes which Joyce said wore like "regular shoes".

Some girls found and wore a saddle shoe style of spike. During the first spring training in Chicago every girl was supposed to take evening charm school classes from a woman named **Helen Rubinstein**. Joyce said she never attended a class and neither did a lot of the girls. The classes were meant for the country girls who management figured "lacked sophistication."No fines or suspensions. The girls were there to play ball. Off the field girls were expected to wear a skirt or dress regardless of the occasion. Once the season ended they could wear what they wanted.

Each team had a chaperone who was either a former player or somebody wishing she was one. Chaperones, or "chappies", had a number of responsibilities but not every day. First of all they dressed like military officers or airline stewardesses Chaperones were in charge of the first aid kit which was often a valuable tool. Cuts, blisters, bruises and strawberries from sliding happened all the time. They also handed out the paychecks and per diem monies on the road and washed and sometimes repaired uniforms on the road. The girls were responsible for their own laundry and repairs while playing at home.

It was the chappies' job to make sure the young man one of the girls wanted to date was reputable. They were also supposed to enforce the curfews after games and be on the lookout for lesbianism since the league frowned on that orientation unlike today. If the chappie was cool, Joyce said, sometimes they would go out with the girls for a drink. Above all they made sure all the girls were wearing a dress or skirt and acted as an intermediary between the girls and the manager.

Racine beat Kenosha and South Bend beat Rockford in the first round of the 1943 best-of-three playoffs. Racine beat South Bend in the finals to win the league's first championship. The Milwaukee Chicks and Minneapolis Millerettes were added to the league in 1944. Both large markets failed miserably in supporting their teams so both moved east after that season, the Chicks to Grand Rapids, Michigan and Millerettes to Fort Wayne, Indiana.

The early salaries ranged between $50 and $85 a week, not bad at all for that time. The girls also got per diem money on the road, $5 a day, which was also pretty good. The money not spent eating was either saved, spent on clothes, underwear or hygiene items. Some sent their money home to help out, others saved for college or a future wedding like Joyce did.

Depending on how many teams were in the league each year the schedule called for between 108-112 games. League play usually began during Memorial Day weekend and finished right after Labor Day. The playoffs kept qualifying teams playing another week. That's potentially 116-118 games in about 100 days. The girls breathed a sigh of relief whenever a game was rained out because it was seldom made up unless it mattered in the standings. There weren't many off days in the schedule the way it was. There was a doubleheader every Sunday plus holidays, just like the men.

In 1945 the game began to change. When Meyerhoff bought out Wrigley's interests the game became a hybrid of fast pitch and baseball. The Rockford Peaches won the first of their four league championships that year. Before the league said good bye to its fast pitch style of play there were some insane numbers posted by **Dorothy Wiltse-Collins** and **Doris Barr.** Wiltse-Collins finished 29-10 for the Daisies in their first season in Fort Wayne in 1945. She struck out 293, threw two no-hitters and posted an earned run average of 0.83. Believe it or not she also tossed 17 shutouts and hit 44 batters. Maybe more unbelievable was that Wiltse-Collins pitched into the 1948 season four months pregnant. She sat out the 1949 season on maternity leave and returned for her final season in 1950. Not only did Canadian **Doris Barr** pitch a no-hitter in 1945 for the Daisies but uncorked 38 wild pitches. She turned 93 on July 29, 2017. The Muskegon Lassies and Peoria Red Wings joined the league in 1946. Spring training was held in Pascagoula, Mississippi on an army base.

During the regular season the South Bend Blue Sox were said to have attracted 10,000 fans to a Fourth of July doubleheader against Kenosha. It was also a big year for the Racine Belles who won their second league championship in four years. The 1947 season got off to a blazing start as all eight teams trained in Havana, Cuba.

The main attraction was not **Jackie Robinson**, who was in the Brooklyn Dodgers camp a short distance away, but **Fredda Thompson Acker**, the 1947 Mrs. America from Anderson, South Carolina. According to her Wikipedia bio Fredda was signed by South Bend for "publicity purposes" only. She signed more autographs than any girl in Cuba as her job was to draw attention to the league. According to her AAGPBL bio Fredda never pitched in a game although it said she threw hard and was good enough to be a contributor. It is not known if she even finished out the season or what she did once her Mrs. America reign ended. All that is known is that Fredda's sister **Viola** actually pitched for the Blue Sox. Fredda died young, 10 days before her 55th birthday, in 1980.

The 1948 season was the pinnacle for the AAGPBL. Not only did the league train in Havana for the second straight year but the Chicago Colleens and Springfield Sallies entered the league giving it 10 teams. In 1948 they were called "developmental teams" which was kind of like Triple-A only they did play against the other eight teams. Both expansion clubs had some good players but not nearly enough. They got pounded a lot.

Chicago finished 47-76 in 1948; Springfield, 41-84. Former big leaguer shortstop **Dave Bancroft** managed the Colleens; former Pirates center fielder **Carson Bybee** the Sallies. In 1949 and 1950 the two teams were dropped from league play but continued to represent the league playing an independent vagabond schedule. They played exhibition games in places like Griffith Stadium in Washington D.C. and Yankee Stadium in New York and rarely played at home.

On the positive side a lot of girls got a chance to play and develop into good players, some good enough to be coveted by the other eight teams. Attendance hit an all-time high of 910,000. Even though the Colleens and Sallies were not very competitive the future looked bright for the AAGPBL. The Grand Rapids Chicks, who won the league championship as the Milwaukee Chicks in 1944, won the championship in 1947. They would win it a third time as a franchise in 1953.

The Peaches developed into a dynasty winning the league championship in 1948, 1949 and 1950 under manager **Bill Allington**. The league was also near the end of its transcendence between fast pitch and baseball. It was written that even though pitching dominated the league a lot of pitchers supposedly had trouble adjusting from fast pitch to sidearm in 1948 and 1949. In 1948 Racine's **Eleanor Dapkus** and Grand Rapids' **Alice Haylett** hurled 10 shutouts each. Twenty pitchers finished with an earned run average of 1.99 or lower. Haylett led the league with .077. There was just one .300 hitter that year, Kenosha's **Audrey Wagner**, .312. Perhaps the real highlight of the season came in the playoffs. South Bend's **Jean Faut** outlasted Haylett 3-2 in 20 innings! Pitching still dominated the 1949 season as nobody batted .300. **Doris Sams** won her second Player of the Year award for batting .279, a 15-10 pitching record and 1.58 ERA. South Bend's **Lillian Faralla** pitched two no-hitters, Faut one.

There were still eight competitive teams but attendance was on its way down. No attendance figure could be found but the trend would continue to go down. Television and the resurgence of major and minor league baseball were said to be the major culprits. The 1950 season proved huge as Meyerhoff told the surviving clubs to seek private ownership and support themselves Perhaps each club would be more effective promoting locally.

The game was headed toward full blown baseball that season. The pitching distance went to 55 feet and base paths to 85 feet. A livelier 10-inch ball was introduced in an effort to jump start the hitting for the fans as pitching continued to dominate the ladies' game. Five hitters batted .300 or better led by **Betty Foss'** .346. Kenosha's **Jean Cione** hurled two no-hitters and teammate **Ruby Stephens** one. Both of Cione's no-nos came in the month of August, one a 12-inning gem.

The Lassies moved from Muskegon, Michigan to Kalamazoo at midseason. It was also the end of the line for the Racine Belles who moved to Battle Creek, Michigan for the 1951 season. With the departure of Meyerhoff the league, which began as a non-profit entity, was now every team for itself. After the league carried 10 teams in 1948 the next three seasons would see it play with eight. In 1949, even though Chicago and Springfield were now traveling teams, they were not counted as part of the league statistically.

After Kenosha and Peoria closed its doors at the end of 1951 the league dropped down to six teams in 1952 and 1953. In 1954, the league's final season, there were just five. In 1943, when nobody really knew what the product would look like on the field, there were just four. Attendance also slid for the third straight year in 1951 although official numbers were not made available. Teams were encouraged to seek more national advertising since operational funds were not all that plentiful. Teams were also told not to give up on local support since attendance revenues barely met the payroll and some not even doing that. It just wasn't there either because of lack of effort or local leadership refusing or unable to help.

South Bend spotted Rockford a 2-0 lead in the finals and then won three straight to win the first of its two straight league championships. Faut was the winner in game three and game five in relief. She also won the first of her two league MVPs that season. **Jane Stoll** had six hits and six RBI in the finals for South Bend. Foss batted .368 for her second straight batting title. The league bid farewell to the Comets and Red Wings at the end of 1951 and there was cause for concern. What franchise would fold next? Joyce was chosen by South Bend in the dispersal draft and eventually signed after a lengthy hold out in the spring of 1952. Joyce was one of the fortunate veterans to gain a roster spot as many girls did not get signed or called it a career and went home. Eighteen players were the most any team could carry. When the league began there were 15 per team.

The National Girls League in Chicago had made an impact on the AAGPBL in that many players jumped to the Chicago circuit for a chance the play or to escape the hectic lifestyle of the AAGPBL. For some it meant playing closer to home, school and getting paid for it, too. The Chicago league was tough. There weren't many rules and players played at their own risk. Many did not play like ladies. It was a tavern league atmosphere if there ever was one. The 1952 season was wild and woolly, especially from South Bend's perspective, as the Blue Sox overcame a tumultuous August to beat Grand Rapids in two games and Rockford in five games of the AAGPBL World Series. One girl was suspended and five others left the ballclub yet the Blue Sox prevailed. Faut had two triples, a double, a total of six hits and three RBI. Joyce had four hits, two walks and four RBI. Other than that there wasn't anything really noteworthy about 1952 except for the Battle Creek Belles relocating to Muskegon after the season.

League attendance continued its free fall and AAGPBL insiders knew the end was in sight. The final two seasons were very competitive come playoff time. 1953 was almost full scale baseball as the base paths were widened to 75 feet and pitching rubber to 56 feet yet according to Wikapedia the changes had "no impact on the game". First-place Fort Wayne beat Kalamazoo 3-1 in the first game of the championship semifinals but the Lassies rebounded to win the next two games 2-1 and 5-3 and the series.

In the other semifinal Rockford crushed the hard-hitting Chicks 9-2 but got badly needed pitching in the latter two games, 5-2 and 4-3. The Chicks won the first two games in the finals also by 5-2 and 4-3 counts as game two was called after seven innings because of cold and rainy weather. It was the third championship for the franchise which started in Milwaukee in 1944. Whereas Battle Creek moved to Muskegon prior to the 1953 season the Belles could not answer the bell in 1954 thus dropping out giving the dying league just five teams going into its final season. It was also the end of the line for Haut who retired with her second league MVP. Perhaps the only true highlight was the league's bats finally woke up. A total of 408 home runs were hit; more than three times more than the previous league high. The pitching rubber was now 60 feet and base paths 85 feet. The ball was now nine inches in circumferences. The fences were also moved in about 20 feet. About as close to real baseball as it got but it was too late.

Joanne Weaver won her third straight batting title with a .429 average, the highest in any professional women's or men's league. The Player of the Year belted 29 home runs and collected 254 total bases. For the second straight year no pitcher won 20 games. South Bend's **Janet Rumsey** won 15 games. Kalamazoo's **Gloria Cordes** pitched 34 straight innings without giving up a run. Kalamazoo, the league's fourth place team at 48-48, won the final league title.

The Lassies, in their fifth and final season in Kalamazoo, beat South Bend two games to one and Fort Wayne topped Grand Rapids two games to none. Kalamazoo, led by Cordes, outlasted Fort Wayne three games to two in the finals. Hard to say if the league had six stable teams in 1955 it might've been able to make a go of it. It was said to be a stretch that the league survived 1954 with just five teams. Another season with five teams or even four was simply out of the question. With attendance heading south in every year since 1949 it came as no surprise the AAGPBL had heard its last hoorahs. The game's top players stuck it out over the last two or three years. You can only play nine at a time and put 18 on a roster. Unfortunately a lot of good players were squeezed out. They either went to the Chicago professional fastpitch league or home where they were legends and heroes on their home town diamonds. The men and women who contributed to the league since 1943 now had their places in baseball history.

A League Of Their Own
Chapter 11

Think about all the baseball or football movies you've seen in your lives. First, let's go all the way back to 1940 when "**Knute Rockne, All-American**" first came out. The movie was about the life of the legendary Notre Dame player and then head coach, played by **Pat O'Brien**. Rockne was about as clean as any athlete and coach ever was but you had to feel sorry for his star running back **George Gipp**, played by **Ronald Reagan**, who was dying of cancer. It spawned the famous line from Rockne, "Tell them to go out there and just win one for the Gipper!". For me the 1942 classic "Pride of the Yankees", starring **Gary Cooper** as **Lou Gehrig** is probably my all-time favorite movie of any kind. One of the humblest men to ever play the game Gehrig found out he had the deadly decease amyotrophic lateral sclerosis. Could you sit there with a straight face and watch him say, "Today I feel like I'm the luckiest man on the face of the earth." in front of a huge Yankee Stadium crowd? Never mind that he played in 2,130 straight games the Lou Gehrig Day speech in 1939 will live forever. You had to feel bad for **Monty Stratton** in the 1949 drama

"The Monty Stratton Story". **Jimmy Stewart** played Stratton, a real life big league pitcher, who shot himself in the lower leg during a hunting accident.

Helped and inspired by his wife Ethel **(June Allyson)** Stratton returned to the major leagues but not without a prosthetic lower leg. He made it back but was never quite the same which was sad. How about the 1957 thriller "Fear Strikes Out"? It's about the early life of Boston Red Sox outfielder **Jimmy Pearsall (Anthony Perkins)** who was pushed hard by his overbearing father **(Karl Malden)** to succeed. Pearsall suffered a mental breakdown and subsequent trip to a mental institution. Many years later in a newspaper interview he told a reporter he was sane and that "he had the papers to prove it". ."Brian's Song" (1971) was the real life story of Chicago Bears rookies **Brian Piccolo (James Caan) and Gale Sayers (Billy Dee Williams**). They were training camp roommates and both ended up making the team, although Piccolo's career and life were being compromised by cancer.

"Bang The Drum Slowly", starring a young **Robert DiNiro** and **Michael Moriarty,** was about the baseball life and decline of catcher **Bruce Pearson** (DiNiro). He is taken to the Mayo Clinic where it is determined he had cancer.

Moriarty played hot-shot pitcher Henry "Arthur" Wigge who held out for more money and insists his new contract contain a clause that Pearson remain on the team for as long as he could. Pearson battles and does just that in the 1973 release. "Eight Men Out" (1988) was about the infamous Chicago Black Sox scandal. The team was said to be divided on throwing the 1919 World Series to the underdog Cincinnati Reds to spite tight wad owner Charles **Comiskey.** Eight players were said to have promised a Chicago bookmaker they would indeed tank the series. No tears in this one. Just lifetime suspensions, denial, cheating and lying. The eight players, including the great **"Shoeless" Joe Jackson**, were banned from major league baseball by new commissioner **Mountain Landis.**

Queen of Diamonds

Speaking of Jackson and his seven banished teammates they appear on **Ray Kinsella's** baseball field in Iowa in "Field of Dreams". "Build it and they will come". Ray Kinsella also gets to finally play catch with his father, John. The 1989 movie might be the greatest sports movie of all time as Kinsella **(Kevin Costner)** discovers his field is not all about baseball. It was the final appearance on the silver screen for the great **Burt Lancaster**. There were a number of subplots and many tears in this one and surprisingly, a lot of criticisms. The only criticism I have is the movie was ruined to some extent as Shoeless Joe Jackson **(Ray Liotta)** was casted as a right handed hitter whereas in real life he was one of the greatest left-handed hitters of his day. "The Babe", (1992), played by **John Goodman**, was not really in the tear jerker category but you had to feel bad for **George Herman Ruth** who was turned over to a Baltimore orphanage by his father. You still felt bad for the Babe to some extent for his life's downfalls and for never getting the Yankees' managerial job. "Cobb" played by **Tommy Lee Jones** (1994) wasn't all that emotional either. The story about **Ty Cobb** was one of the rare movies in which you kept waiting for something negative to happen to one of the game's greatest hitters and finally did. Perhaps the greatest player ever, at least statistically, was never loved or admired by anybody. In fact, he might have been the most hated for his many dirty tactics. That brings us to the movie seemingly everybody loves, "A League Of Their Own". Even though the movie was sugar coated by Hollywood how could you not love and root for the girls who were trying to survive in a men's game? "There is no crying in baseball!" yelled **Tom Hanks'** character, **Jim Dugan**. Well, unless you're a guy wearing a baseball uniform on the field I would disagree with that.

The movie, directed by **Penny Marshall**, was a great movie because it made us cry or at least tear up in a number of places. It made us stand up and cheer and be angry at Jim Dugan and anybody else who posed a threat to the girls. It made us cheer for the Rockford

Peaches whether we liked them or not. We fell in love with the girls and what they brought to the game. You just knew Kit **(Lori Petty)** was going to get the better of older sister Dottie **(Geena Davis)** in their sibling rivalry. You felt bad for **Betty "Spaghetti" Horn** when she was told in the clubhouse by manager Dugan in front of the team her husband had been killed in the war.

We may not have known Dottie and her husband drove back to Oregon when he returned from the war but we probably did not know the couple would turn around and return to Rockford just in time for the playoffs. Dottie Hinson was considered the league's best player. Kit, traded to Racine during the regular season, gets the best of Dottie in a collision at home plate causing Dottie to drop the ball as Racine won the league's first championship. The once great Jim Dugan, a fictional character, is an alcoholic and is tough on the girls in the beginning. As the movie progresses Dugan actually becomes understanding and tolerant of the girls.

The movie had its light moments. Let's not forget the cigar chomping scout **Ernie Capadino**. Mr. Warmth and Charm he was not. Or how about Dottie calling Jim Dugan "a big lush" or flashing signs to the third base coach while Dugan tried to do the same from the dugout drunk? Remember the homely **Marla Hooch** going out to a bar with the girls wearing a dress? Or singing karaoke? Or marrying a guy she met at the bar and showing up to a reunion with him 40 years later? How about Dottie catching a foul pop up behind her back or **Madonna** catching a ball doing the splits as the flash bulbs went off? And let's not forget the founder of the league, "**Walter Harvey**", ala **Phillip K. Wrigley**, played by Penny Marshall's brother, **Garry**.

Woman or not you had to stand up and cheer for the girls even if they struck out. As I said earlier in this book it was a men's game and a men's business but it was the girls' time to shine.

The powers that be wanted the girls to look and act like ladies yet were treated like men. I wonder how long this league could have lasted had the girls been treated with some dignity and respect. The stronger, more mature players survived. Remember the end of the movie when the real players met and reminisced? **Joyce Westerman** was one of them. "They sent us all a letter telling us they were going to make a movie." said Joyce. "So they told us to go to Skokie, Illinois if we were interested. Forty-nine of us showed up. Madonna was there. Our part in the movie would be shot at the Hall of Fame." Even while writing this book I had to stop and wipe away some tears when I discovered what life in the All-American Girls Professional Baseball League was truly about. To Joyce its been all about family: her real family and AAGPBL family. "It was about building our first house our two kids and grandkids." said Joyce. She remembers being on a bowling alley and golf course not more than "once in my life" "I was very family-oriented." she said.

It was a huge thrill for Joyce not only having her name inscribed on a bronze plaque in the Hall of Fame but having a silent and brief appearance in the movie. And to have her family there for both of them. Years ago when Joyce and I first met I saw the movie again and it was then the tears ran down my cheeks for the first time near the end. I felt real happiness for not only Joyce but the other girls who were there. Even during the movie I felt like standing and cheering every time a good play was made or something good happened to any of the girls. **Roger Ebert**, who has reviewed and critiqued more than a few movies in his day, had this to say about "A League of their Own": "(Penny) Marshall shows her women characters in a tug-of-war between new images and old values, and so her movie was about transition – about how it felt as a woman suddenly to have new roles and freedom. The movie has a bittersweet charm. The baseball sequences we've seen before. What's fresh are the personalities of the players, the gradual unfolding of their coach and the way this early chapter of women's liberation fit into the hide bound traditions of professional baseball. By the end, when the women get together again for their reunion, its touching the way they have to admit that, whaddaya know, they really were pioneers."

Let's forget about baseball for a moment and think about what playing in the league meant to these girls. Many of them went back to school and became not just teachers but good teachers. Just as many became not just parents and grandparents but good ones. Some of them became entrepreneurs. Many found other ways to make a living. Still many of them married and raised families like Joyce. In others words: Most of the girls went on to become better people. They weren't all great ballplayers but turned out to be successful human beings.

The war years, during which the All-American Girls Baseball League existed, taught us all something besides baseball. I believe it taught us all how to persist. Joyce doesn't go to reunions alone. Her two daughters and at least four of her granddaughters go, too. I can only imagine what the movie means to Joyce. Both of her daughters were athletic, educated and are still teaching school. So are the granddaughters. College just wasn't an option for Joyce who lived her life the hard way and succeeded at every crossroad she encountered. Her daughters and grandchildren are for the better because of her.

They Said It
Chapter 12

"Every day after practice (1943) Mr. Wrigley sent us to Helena Rubinstein's charm school to learn how to put on make-up, to put on a coat and to get in and out of a car or chair. Back at the hotel he made us wear skirts. If you dressed in slacks you had to use the servants' elevator. – Lillian Jackson

"They were selling a product. They wanted us to be feminine and at the same time play like DiMaggio. What they didn't realize is how well the girls could actually play" – Sophie Kurys

"…..once they (fans) saw how well we played ball they were hooked. We even stayed with families the first five to seven years. They treated us like members of their family. They would invite us over to dinner and give us presents. And the kids would ask us for our autographs!" – Dottie Schroeder

"At first they came out to see the girls. But we won them over with good baseball". – Dottie Kamenshek

"We will select the kind of players that people will want to see in action. Then we will groom them to make sure they are acceptable." – Phillip K. Wrigley

"Every day was exciting to me." – Bonnie Baker

"I don't think we'll ever see anything like it again." – Dorothy Hunter

"When we were playing we didn't realize what we had. We were just a bunch of young kids doing what we liked best. But most of us recognize now that those were the most meaningful days of our lives."– Dottie Wiltse-Collins

"We would rather play ball than eat. We put our hearts and souls into the league. We thought it was our job to do our best because we were the All-American girls. We felt like we were keeping up our country's morale. – LaVonne "Pepper" Paire

"Femininity is the keynote of our league; no pants-wearing, tough-talking female ballplayer will play on any of our (four) teams."– Max Carey, President of the AAGPBL and a manager

"What gets me is these pitchers nowadays. If you get six innings out of them they think they're wonderful. We had girls who sometimes pitched 19, 20 innings!"– Earlene Risinger

"OK, let's make like a bread truck and haul buns, ladies!" – Doris Murphy from the movie

"I'd pay $50,000 for her (Dottie Schroeder) if she were a boy." – former Cubs manager Charley Grimm

"We had some glamour pusses, but most of us were just white collar girls who stopped wearing collars. Me, I'm strictly the fresh, wholesome type. If the customers were interested in legs instead of arms you'd never see me in the line up." – A former player who wished to remain anonymous

"If you were hurt you played hurt. I broke my thumb one time and the doctor said, 'you're done for six weeks'. Four nights later I was catching." – Magdalena Redman

Beast mode – When in a state of serious training or at a high level of effort. – Carl Valle March 4, 2004

"Of course it's hard! It's supposed to be hard! If it was easy everybody would do it! Hard is what makes it great!" – Tom Hanks' character Jim Dugan

"There is no crying in baseball!" – Tom Hanks' character Jim Dugan

Joyce (Westerman) and I were sitting in church waiting for the service to begin when I said to her, "You know Joyce. When you played against Jimmie Foxx's Fort Wayne Daisies Double X was looking right at you when you were holding one of his runners on first base and he was coaching third base! I know you weren't thinking about it at the time but that had to be so cool!" A little smile appeared on Joyce's lips, the kind that looked like the cat swallowed the canary, as she said, 'I'll tell you what's cooler than that. We're both in the Hall of Fame." – Randy Donais

Randy Donais

Dear Randy July 20, 2017

I think it is wonderful that you have undertaken the tremendous job of writing a book about Joyce Westerman.

She is a lovely person and I enjoyed being in her company. Spending more time with her would have been my pleasure. The reason we did not is my fault. I had a little boy to take care of and a house to keep clean.

She was a great ballplayer and I admired her moves at first base. I will never forget her.

Sincerely,
Jean Faut

More Facts And Numbers
Chapter 13

Joyce Hill-Westerman statistics
Year G AB R H 2B 3B HR RBI SB BB SO BA
1945 9 18 0 2 0 0 0 0 0 0 0 .111
1946 21 57 6 7 0 0 0 3 7 9 12 .123
1947 90 251 24 57 5 2 0 19 16 36 26 .227
1948 89 252 29 47 6 5 0 28 18 43 37 .187
1949 64 121 16 23 1 2 0 12 4 32 12 .190
1950 70 197 26 50 4 2 0 19 4 45 29 .254
1951 102 355 51 86 12 3 0 50 20 68 19 .242
1952 86 264 39 73 5 0 0 36 12 59 14 .277

AAGPBL teams Joyce played for
1945 Grand Rapids Chicks
1946 South Bend Blue Sox, Fort Wayne Daisies
1947 Peoria Red Wings
1948 Peoria Red Wings, Racine Belles
1949 Racine Belles

1950 Peoria Red Wings
1951 Peoria Red Wings
1952 South Bend Blue Sox

Teams that played in the All-American Girls Softball League (1943-1948), All-American Girls Professional Baseball League (1949-1950), American Girls Baseball League (1951-1954)

Overall, it is known as the All-American Girls Professional Baseball League.

The teams that played in the league
Rockford Peaches, 1943-1954
South Bend Blue Sox, 1943-54
Racine Belles, 1943-1950
Kenosha Comets, 1943-1951
Milwaukee Chicks, 1944
Grand Rapids Chicks, 1945-1954
Minneapolis Millerettes, 1944
Fort Wayne Daisies, 1945-1954
Muskegon Lassies, 1946-1949
Peoria Red Wings, 1946-1951
Chicago Colleens, 1948
Springfield Sallies, 1948
Kalamazoo Lassies, 1950-1954
Battle Creek Belles, 1951-1952
Muskegon Belles, 1953

League champions
1943 – Racine Belles
1944—Milwaukee Chicks
1945—Rockford Peaches
1946—Racine Belles
1947—Grand Rapids Chicks

1948—Rockford Peaches
1949—Rockford Peaches
1950—Rockford Peaches
1951—South Bend Blue Sox
1952—South Bend Blue Sox
1953—Grand Rapids Chicks
1954—Kalamazoo Lassies

Women's Athletic Hall of Fame
1999—Claire Schillace
2002—Fay Dancer
2003—Dorothy Ferguson-Key
2005—Joanne Winter
2010—Dorothy Kamenshek
2012—Jean Faut, Doris Sams
2013—Yvonne Paire, Sophie Kurys

Rockford won four of the 12 league championships. Milwaukee/Grand Rapids won three; Racine and South Bend, two; and Kalamazoo, one. Rockford and South Bend were the only franchises to last all 12 seasons. The Minneapolis Millerettes and Milwaukee Chicks lasted just one year at their original locations. The Millerettes moved to Fort Wayne, Indiana and became the Daisies and the Chicks moved to Grand Rapids, Michigan starting in 1945. The Chicago Colleens and Springfield Sallies lasted three years as developmental and then traveling teams before disbanding after the 1950 season.

Bill Francis eats, sleeps and drinks the All-American Girls Professional Baseball League in its section of Baseball's Hall of Fame. The former sportswriter maintains the website, statistics, and facts and is eager to help a student or whoever with research on some aspect of the league. He is responsible some of the quotes in this book as is **Troy Farkas**. **Jeneane Lesko** wrote a lengthy piece about the history of the league from which I retrieved a ton of information. The piece was edited by **Jean Cione**, **Sue Macy** and **Merrie Fidler**. **Jim Sargeant** wrote a number of the girls' biographies.

Two key books were also huge in the writing of this book. **The Dutiful Dozen** was written in 1997 by **W.C. Madden** and published by Madden Publishing Company, Noblesville, Indiana. There is a lot more detail as to Joyce's 1952 season with the South Bend Blue Sox than what I am providing here. Also, **Joyce Westerman: Baseball Hero**, was written by **Bob Kann** as part of the Badger Biography Series in 2012 and published by the Wisconsin Historical Society Press. Joyce detests the tag of Baseball Hero but the book is a decent read.

Usurps from The Kenosha Comets, written by **John W. Bailey** of Carthage College, also found its way into this book. It contains a lot of facts during the Comets' nine-year stay in Kenosha. It was published by Badger Press in Kenosha in 1997. Much of the information was also derived from the Kenosha News archives.

Joanna Rachel Turner, who was a high school junior in 1976, wrote a phenomenal paper on the beginnings of the league which was submitted to the Chicago Metro History Fair and placed in the top 100 entries out of about 2,000. She is an Evanston, Illinois native and graduate of Cornell University in New York. I used some of the quotes she gathered in this book. **Jeff Shannon** of Amazon.com is also an AAGPBL contributor whose quotes I also used. Also thanks to the Kenosha County Historical Society, **Jennie Tunkieicz** in Kenosha County Executive **Jim Kreuser's** office and **David Backmann**.

Some Final Thoughts
Chapter 14

After spending dozens of hours with **Joyce Westerman** on the creation of this book I do not believe I ever talked more baseball with one person than her. Any way you slice it Joyce is a total and complete success. Now there are and were those who grew up poor during the Depression and war years and battled their way back to success. As it was said many times in the past, "Successful people do what unsuccessful people won't." Sometimes fear is a key motivator.

Joyce is undoubtedly the toughest little woman I ever met. That could be said about a lot of people but it most definitely was Joyce. She worked hard to achieve the goals and things she always wanted, especially a place in professional baseball, once unheard of for women. Everything else took care of itself. Joyce was raised during the Great Depression but has made a great life for herself because she worked hard to make one. She isn't drowning in wealth or public attention but is rich in family and friends. If any of you girls or young women reading this book desire to be something more than what you are then Joyce Westerman is your blue print.

The All-American Girls Professional Baseball League was a spring board for those hopes and desires. It was one of those things that proved dreams do come true if one were willing to pay the price. Ask any of the girls who played in the league. It was a liberating experience. "Aside from my family it was the best thing that ever happened to me." Joyce said. She was an average player in the AAGPBL and had to work hard to be that. She didn't bring great natural talent to the table but brought her Kenosha work ethic and toughness into a fledging league that needed it. Joyce's work ethic is the same today as when she was a child performing farm chores when she wasn't going to school. Her willingness to work hard got her into the league and kept her there.

At 91 how many seniors mow their lawn or shovel their driveways like Joyce is willing to do? That's work ethic that can't be taught today. Either you have it or you don't. The All-American Girls Professional Baseball League simply minded the store until baseball's stars returned from the wars. It had a personality and flair of its own yet the baseball purists could not wait until the major league stars returned. The AAGPBL offered good softball/baseball played by young ladies who looked and acted like ladies. Even though Joyce went with the program she played the game the way it was meant to be played – all out on every pitch. Or as she calls it, "desire".

Joyce lives for her family and after 65 years still lives for the AAGPBL. She's only missed three reunions in 36 years. Her daughters and granddaughters go to every one. The league will forever have its place in baseball history and lore. Joyce was a part of that history and lore. She was always available to help out on reunions. She is still a giver just like she was on the field. But like a dear friend or family member who passes away there were certainly some tears from the former players and fans when the league closed its doors after the 1954 season.

Queen of Diamonds

Ask Joyce. Her eight years were worth all the long hours of work, the injuries, the long bus rides and the tough losses. She handled it all as well as could be expected while others took their ball and went home. She made some decent money, enough to help build her first house with husband Ray. But money wasn't really what it was all about. It was a big step forward for girls and women. "If we can do it you can do it!"

Today every high school and college has a fast pitch team. Back in the forties and early fifties there were virtually none. You had to play in a county or city league. Joyce Westerman has lived a long and successful life and the AAGPBL was only part of it. And what a huge part. "I was just thrilled to be there." she said. "It was a dream come true."

Before I close I would like to leave you with my three favorite baseball trivia questions.

1. Except for a couple of war years and season-long injury this man pitched between 1934 and 1952. He is the only pitcher to face Babe Ruth, Lou Gehrig, Joe DiMaggio and Mickey Mantle in regular season games.
2. He is the only man to pitch in a World Series. Years later he would also umpire in one. Hint: He pitched for the Yankees and his son was a journeyman infielder in the major leagues in the 1990's. One of the teams the son played for was the Milwaukee Brewers.
3. Twenty-seven men hit 500 home runs or more in the major leagues. Who had the highest lifetime batting average and who had the lowest?
4. Of the 27 men in the 500 Home Run Club which one is still playing?

1. Al Benton. (Johnny Sain said he pitched to Ruth and Mantle in exhibition games.)
2. Bill Kunkel (His son is Jeff Kunkel).
3. Ted Williams, .344; Harmon Killibrew, .256.
4. Albert Pujols.

Twenty-year-old Joyce with the South Bend Blue Sox in 1946.

Joyce with her Dad and Mom, Cecil and Lillian Hill, at Horlick Field in Racine in 1948.

Joyce (back row, far left) with the Peoria Red Wings in 1947.

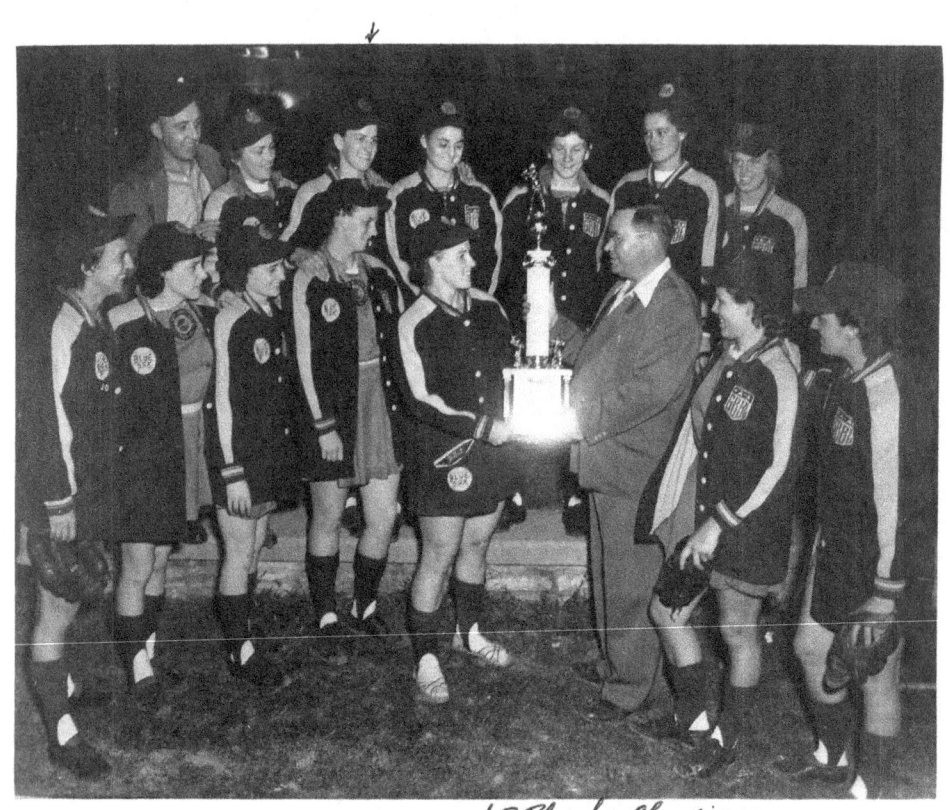

Trophy presentation in Freeport, Illinois to the 1952 league champion Blue Sox. Joyce is in the back row, second girl from the left. It was Joyce's last game in the AAGPBL.

Queen of Diamonds

Rookie Joyce Hill with the 1945 Grand Rapids Chicks.

Joyce as a member of the Blue Sox in 1946.

Joyce demonstrates the "dirt in the skirt" slide into third base. (The year, team and third baseman are unknown).

The Kenosha Comets first home, Lakefront Stadium in 1945.

Joyce is holding a runner on at first base as a member of the Blue Sox in 1952.

Some of the AAGPBL girls who landed in Havana, Cuba in either 1947 or 1948 for spring training. Joyce is in the first row seventh from the left.

Joyce (far right) enjoys some girl time with her Peoria Red Wings teammates in April, 1947.

Maggie Russo takes a cut in this undated photo taken at Simmons Field in Kenosha.

Joyce and her new husband Ray Westerman in Peoria, 1951.

Peoria teammate Maggie Russo, Ray Westerman and Joyce in Peoria, 1951.

A young Joyce on the family tractor with her Dad, Cecil Hill, and two of her sisters.

Joyce washing her first car in 1946.

Joyce sitting on her riding mower in her Kenosha yard.

JOYCE HILL
catcher - first base - outfield

 82

Born: 12/29/25
Kenosha, WI
Height: 5'5"
Weight: 150
Batted: Left
Threw: Right

BATTING RECORD

YEAR	TEAM	G	AB	R	H	2B	3B	HR	RBI	SB	BB	SO	AVG
1945	Grand Rapids	9	18	0	2	No Stats Available							.111
1946	S.Bend/Ft. Wayne	21	57	6	7	0	0	0	3	7	9	12	.123
1947	Peoria	90	251	24	57	5	2	0	19	16	36	26	.227
1948	Peoria/Racine	89	252	29	47	6	5	0	28	18	43	37	.187
1949	Racine	64	121	16	23	1	2	0	12	4	32	12	.190
1950	Peoria	70	197	26	50	4	2	0	19	4	45	29	.254
1951	Peoria	102	355	51	86	13	3	0	50	20	68	19	.242
1952	South Bend	86	264	39	73	5	0	0	36	12	59	14	.277
Total		531	1515	191	345	34	14	0	167	81	292	149	.228

Joyce played on the 1952 South Bend championship team. This 8-year veteran was a steady performer, at bat or as either starting catcher or first baseman.

© 1995 Larry Fritsch Cards
Official Baseball Card Of The AAGPBL - Players Association

Queen of Diamonds

This is one of Joyce's baseball cards. It is uncertain as to when the actual picture was taken but it was part of a set made by Larry Fritsch Baseball Cards in 1995.

The Victory Song

Batter up! Hear that call!
The time has come for one and all
To play ball!
We are the members of the All-American league.
We come from cities near and far!
We've got Canadians, Irishmen and Swedes,
We're all for one and one for all,
We're All-Americans!
Each girl stands, her head so proudly high!
Her motto, "Do or die"!
She's not the one to use or need an alibi,
Our chaperones are not too soft,
They're not too tough!
Our managers are on the ball,
We have a president who really knows his stuff!
We're all for one and one for all,
We're All-Americans!

www.ingramcontent.com/pod-product-compliance
Lightning Source LLC
Chambersburg PA
CBHW071518080526
44588CB00011B/1477